Marriage
is the first step
toward divorce

Marriage is the first step toward divorce

BY

Pamela Mason

WITH VI WOLFSON

PAUL S. ERIKSSON, INC.
NEW YORK, N.Y.

This is for dear Dr. Leon Krohn who delivers the
best part of many a marriage including mine!

NOTE: At the date of writing, all the happy Hollywood marriages mentioned in this book were intact. But we must disclaim responsibility for any changes which may occur before we can be rushed into print because, as we all know, marriage is. . . .

P.M.
V.W.

Contents

CONTENTS

Marriage
is the first step
toward divorce

1 { MARRIAGE IS FOR
NUTS AND BOLTS

Sometimes very peculiar people get married. Most
of them are harmless but many of them shouldn't
marry at all, but they do for selfish reasons and
unwholesome ones. Their nut-and-bolt-iness ranges
from the mildly eccentric to the wildly fantastic
with all possible variations between. On the mild
side there's the case of my own grandfather who just
couldn't resist a new house every six months. (Of
course I'm referring to a *residence*.) He'd go out to
work in the morning, on the way see a house that
struck his fancy, rent it and come home that evening to tell my grandmother they were moving
again. In their ten years of marriage I believe my
grandparents moved twenty-two times. She nearly
went mad and when finally he died of throat cancer

aggravated by alcohol, she said, "Well, thank heavens we shan't have to move this year!"

Though they have to be classed under nuts and bolts, Mamas' boys really aren't such a bad lot, matrimonially speaking. There are quite a few of these men who hibernate until their mothers die or reach the ripe old age when death is on its way. Then they decide to get married, either because Mother wants to see them settled comfortably with someone who will clean the house, or because they've become afraid to be left without some sort of mother. Most of these men are normal males—although other men always suspect the ones who stay with Mummy for an unusually long time. Actually this sort of boy may have plenty of girl friends—somehow there's never a girl shortage—or one particular friend who is waiting it out with bright, eager eyes. It isn't easy for him to replace good old Mother in all the wonderful things she did for him, and he is apt to compare most women unfavorably with her, especially if he's over fifty. Yet, most likely, he will make a successful adjustment to marriage because he's accustomed to having a woman in the house to fuss over him when he comes home and he's going to keep that going for him with one wife or another until the day he dies. Therefore Mothers' boys are pretty safe bets in the marriage business. Usually they can support a wife solidly and if by chance she should leave, they will soon have another try at it. You can count on it— no Mother's boy ever will be left a miserable old bachelor with nobody to keep his hearth warm.

Not many women are lucky enough to snare such well housebroken men. Many husbands are completely inconsiderate, even cruel. A British actress friend of mine who has appeared on TV and in films here, remarried a few years ago after several previous marital fizzles. When I saw her some time later, she seemed terribly exhausted and rather hysterical, and told me she'd been ill before her marriage and still needed some rest. But her new husband was a dynamic and restless man who kept her up most of the night drinking and talking. After four hours of sleep, which was all he ever needed, he would insist she get up to fix his breakfast. Then he, a writer, would work for a few hours at his typewriter and for the balance of the day, listen to music or relax in some way pleasing to himself— but he wouldn't let my friend go back to bed. If she tried to sneak upstairs and lie down, he would come racing in and jeer at her, "What's the matter with you? Are you an invalid? Get up and show some life!"

The story didn't surprise me for I had sized up the man when we met. I thought he looked like a bully and naturally the person he could bully the easiest would be a small woman. I think such a man uses the woman he marries to take out his hostilities on so that he doesn't have to compete in a world he probably isn't fitted to compete in. At any rate, my friend is unwilling to face another marriage failure and so she's trying to stick it out, no doubt at the cost of her health.

In the same category as that man, but actually much worse, is the famous swashbuckling actor I'd always considered quite attractive and charming—until one evening when I was invited, for the first time, to his home. With his wife and other guests we had watched a film and, after the lights came on, sat around discussing it. All at once I heard the actor yelling at the lady (his make-up man's wife) sitting next to him. "You're the kind of woman," he was shouting at the top of his voice, "who causes all this puritannical nonsense! You're a—— and a——." The woman was very patient and calm. "All I said was, I think it's desirable that a twelve-year-old girl should avoid being pregnant as long as possible."

He began raving like a madman. "How unnatural! How filthy! Your kind of woman denies nature, you——" He was using the vilest language I have ever heard in public and shaking his finger practically in the poor woman's eyes while her husband stood, white and paralyzed, unable to defend her for fear of losing his job. To my mind the whole incredible scene could only be accounted for by the actor's being roaring drunk.

I spoke to his wife. "He must have had some powerful drinks." And she said, "Oh no, he never drinks." "But what about—?" I gestured toward the frenzied man. "Oh," she explained, "that woman just irritates him."

There was no doubt of that. When I was making my escape, at the same time the other couple left, I saw the actor running after their car, still yelling profanely and winding up with a hard kick at the rear fender. I ask you, could anything be nuttier or boltier than that?

Under the heading of peculiar people who marry must come the homosexual. What motivates a homosexual to get married? Usually, I presume, it's a try at respectability and at pulling the wool over the world's eyes. Less often it might be the result of an attempt to go straight and a sincere belief in the possibility. Rarely it may be because the homosexual, at the time he marries, doesn't realize he is that way.

The majority of homosexual marriages must be very unhappy for the woman. It's a rough discovery for a normal female to find herself married to a man who has a faggy friend and isn't really interested in her at all. If she doesn't realize at the time of the wedding what the homosexual is and why he married her, when she eventually finds out, she may become neurotic, even suicidal, learning that she's walked into something she can't possibly handle. On the other hand, if she knows just what she is getting into and doesn't mind, it might be she is madly in love with him and refuses to accept the fact he is the way he is. Just as women who marry alcoholics, drug addicts and murderers think once they have him in hand, he'll be different. (I think it's pretty safe to say, he never is.) Or the woman might be marrying to escape, either from bitter past experiences with other men or from sex itself.

I believe many women aren't seeking husbands as husbands. They're seeking marriages as marriages. Marriage to such a woman represents income— unearned—and freedom from certain responsibilities. It gives her back in fact the nostalgic situation of living at home, being protected by dear old Dad's prestige. If this woman wants no more out of life than a home, respectability and acceptance, then any man is better than no man. In fact a homosexual may be much better for her because all he wants from her is the cover-up as she does from him, an ideal relationship for both. Also, this relationship makes no further demands on her than dear old Dad did.

Some women actually seem to seek out homosexuals for marriage. I once employed a rather pretty woman who was married to an out-and-out fairy hairdresser who lisped and carried on exactly as they all do. When she confided in me that she was unhappy and was headed for a divorce, I deliberately asked her, "Isn't he a homosexual?" And she said, "No, not at all. Quite the reverse! But I just can't stand him. He bores me." This baffled me because he seemed quite the swish. I was convinced of it after they got their divorce and she immediately became infatuated with another fairy who worked at the studio; he was blatantly queer, even to having his hair dyed blonde in front. For some reason that woman was terribly drawn to unmanly men.

This occurs even in Hollywood's high places. A one time famous film actress has been married—apparently quite happily—to two homosexuals. After she was widowed by the first one, she found another—just as abnormal—to take his place.

Then there was the young and lovely widow of a famous tough executive in the motion picture business. He had been a bit of a hound, to say the least —as are most husbands. She had been a good woman who probably reserved her real living for after his trip to the hereafter. Once he'd reached the point of no return and she was certain he couldn't come popping back at an embarrassing moment, she really let fly and took a look around the world. Several brief romances and one quickie marriage later, she took up with a celebrated homosexual, one who obviously hadn't much else on his queer little mind. This was the great love of her life because, she said, he was more interesting, more charming and more fun than anyone in her experience. Also, she insisted he was much more adequate physically than other men. Most people who knew him doubted that because this fellow practically wore a lace collar and flew through the air on his own trapeze. The romance went on successfully for years, so it must be assumed she was happier with him than she had been while married to the bad man who really was a man.

To me it seems unthinkable that a female could be happy with one of those misfits who feels nothing but contempt for women. During a television interview with a whole flock of queenly hairdressers, David Susskind asked one of them, "What do you think of the ladies who come to your shop when you see them looking their very worst, their hair wound in curlers?" The fag, all dressed up in a belted fur coat, simpered, "I've never met a woman I couldn't hate!"

On the other side of the page, there is the case of one of our most famous actresses who had a big movie magazine type of marriage. This romantic idyll finally was broken up by another woman, and our heroine was much pitied by the public. However, insiders claim that her dear sweet face covers the Boy of Our Day. They say the fellow she was married to—supposed to be average and normal—really was a winsome little creature, and she, who looked the winsome little creature, actually was quite a fellow. In cases like this you really can't identify the players without a program.

It's been said there are hundreds of thousands of married women who are actively homosexual. Usually they are unsuspected because it's more difficult to spot this oddity in a woman. Many of these lad-like ladies marry deliberately because they are homosexual. This gives them a chance not only to get away from their parental homes but also the freedom to meet and pursue other women. The men they marry supply them with upkeep and give them little bother. It's not difficult after a while, as these women know, to keep a man at arm's length simply by laughing at him. Men need a great deal of food for their ego. No matter how secure in other ways, eventually a man can be put out of the marital bed with the use of sheer mirth. I think this trick has been used on many men who now are supporting large homes while the wife carries on with her bridge club. The cuckold goes on innocently handing out the cash, convinced that his wife merely has an overdeveloped sense of humor.

Some of these women, however, can pull off the

act more easily because they are bi-sexual rather than completely homosexual. I have in mind the case of a woman who is married to a famous comedian and carries on her little affairs with "les" girls without her husband's being even slightly suspicious. She gives him all he wants or needs from a wife. What she does when he is away on one of his many night club tours doesn't concern him at all. Though he furnishes her with unlimited wealth, making her role of wife palatable enough for her to play the complicated game, somehow I don't believe she's happy. But in his case, ignorance really seems to result in bliss.

You can find many strange deviations in married people. I happen to be quite strait-laced myself about such things. I didn't know the basically lewd facts of life until I was over thirty and a mother, probably because I was so carefully raised and nurtured in England. I thought there was just one thing married people did to each other and that it always was done quite simply. I didn't understand there were about a hundred thousand different positions. I never wanted to understand it, and I still don't. However, I must say, just once I had a bitter shock. A gentleman was courting me and we were having one of those average chases around the living room, during which I was squeaking, "I really don't know you well enough!" when suddenly he slashed off his belt. Appalled and terrified, I realized he was about to give me a whipping. He was a man I'd been working with, who, I thought, was just a good clean married man trying to cheat on his wife. Imagine my horror upon discovering he not only cheated but had a belt fetish! You can be sure I got him out of the house in a hurry and never let him through the door again. I thought I was the only woman in the world who'd had such a terrifying experience until I mentioned it to some of my girl friends and they assured me, "Oh, that's a very common thing!"

Later I learned that one of my closest friends—a great celebrity—was a pathological masochist who insisted that any man who romanced her must, first of all, be good with his fists. Her favorite colors seemed to be black and blue, preferably all over her body. (But not of course as high as shoulder level because she liked to wear low cut dresses.) Most of us don't care for that kind of cuddling but some women seem to have a peculiar notion there's something masculine about brutality and something feminine about passive receivership. I'm sure this goes on within many marriages.

I have another friend who married an attractive, wealthy young man when she was an attractive young girl. He courted her very nicely, but after they were married she soon realized there was something wrong, though she couldn't figure out what. He was quite rude and sadistic to her verbally, making her life as miserable as possible. Then came the day when he waltzed in, carrying a very large pair of black silk stockings and suggested she put them on. My friend was amazed that he should buy her such oversized hose until she realized they would fit him. From then on she had some strange suspicions about him. One day when he wasn't in his office, she peeked into his desk drawers and found he had stashed there a large collection of ladies' underwear, all in his own size. My friend was too shy and inhibited and horrified to do anything so she suffered silently for another few years by which time they both hated each other. She, because she knew of the apparel on his mind, and he, frustrated because he couldn't put on his undies and prance around the bedroom. Of course they divorced. To this day I'm not sure exactly what he was but I presume it was a special kind of transvestite.

To investigate thoroughly the peculiarities in a marriage, you'd have to form a very close friendship with either the husband or wife. Even at that you couldn't be sure you were getting an accurate picture for, naturally, each one would clean up his own part in the mess. I don't know if the physical craziness or the emotional madness is predominant in most of the nuts-and-bolts arrangements. I suspect the emotional ones have the edge, but you hear less about them. One thing is certain—people who are using each other in marriage for the wrong purposes will come a nasty cropper sooner or later.

2 { MARRIAGE IS FOR YOUNG AND OLD

I have an idea marriage would be more successful if it became customary for opposites—age-wise—to mate. Actually there's a certain rightness in this idea. You can go back to the Bible and find that in ancient times, an old tired cold King had two beautiful virgins put into bed beside him to keep him warm—like human hot water bottles. (Exactly in what way they *really* kept him warm was not stated, but we can make a few shrewd guesses.) However, nobody seems to remember this in regard to the ever-increasing marriages between older men and younger girls.

There always has been a tendency for younger women, looking for material security, to be attracted to father figures. A girl would discover a man who was in a good position, had a nice car, probably a substantial insurance policy. His children by his previous marriage were grown, so he was on his own, rather sad and depleted by life and very appreciative of the young woman's attention. And she would think, *oh gosh, if daddy had only been like this!*

That's what I used to think was back of it all—nothing more. Having lived and learned somewhat, now I realize there are a lot more things in favor of such a relationship. Apart from the Biblical example, there are many peculiar biological and sexual facts that suggest this is the right way for life to end. It's absurd to assume that an elderly man and an elderly woman are going to get much kick out of each other in any way except as friends. But an elderly man, flattered and respected by a young girl, and a young girl, admired and adored by an elderly man, may find themselves having a perfect relationship.

Obviously it isn't going to be a permanent relationship because the old man won't live as long as the young girl. Eventually, if she has a family by him, she may find she must bring the children up alone. Generally though the elderly man's wealth or insurance will make it possible for the young girl to afford a young man after "daddy" is gone.

It seems to me there are important reasons that

18

justify this particular deviation, if deviation it is. Men, as they get older, don't necessarily lose their *entire* power for making love. Certainly they don't lose their urge because that's all in the mind. But they do slacken off a lot from about forty onward, depending on the energy of the man and the kind of life he's led. Often such men need more than the usual stimulation to get them off the ground.

An elderly wife who's been around a long time and who is a familiar figure finds it hard to supply that unusual inspiration, whereas a young girl, with a sweet look of love in her eyes and a complete ignorance of the act of love, is going to be inspiring, indeed, to a man who takes a good deal of time to get going.

The normal, sensitive, emotional young girl is sexually unaware until she's been awakened. Many women aren't completely awakened until after they've had a child because this promotes glandular function. But the innocent girl, not entirely ready for love, is much more likely to be stirred by the slow effort of an older man than by the quick and frantic lovemaking of a young man.

The average young man knows practically nothing about love or about women but he is consumed with a great sexual urge which will drive him into any female, or even a watermelon—practically anything he can find—if he's an energetic fellow. The older man, having a tough time getting going, can take all the hours a young girl needs. He can gaze into her eyes; he can stroke her arm or pat her hand; he can tell her how wonderful she is (and all the while be wondering if he will be able to do anything at all with her.)

If he finds he can, of course the kick is unbelievable. He's so pleased that his power has come back —not exactly in the same vibrant proportions of his youth but at least it's active. As a result he loves her far more than any unappreciative clout could. (A young man doesn't have to thank a girl for having made him into a man again.) The older man is grateful to her for having brought back his vigor and given him the feeling that he is a master of life. And he is sure the whole world envies him because she's young, proving he must have been a heck of a guy to get her.

The young girl meanwhile has many advantages to consider. She needn't worry about living in a dingy two-room apartment—only a very foolish young girl would marry a *poor* older man. He's going to pour jewels and furs and clothes on her as he never did on his first wife. At the same time, she is escaping from the hideous fate of being pushed around in a bed day and night by a lusty young fellow who will make her pregnant practically every time he looks at her—for, with the other man, she is fairly safe in this respect. Of course there are rare exceptions to this rule. For example, Charlie Chaplin raised about eight children with Oona (only because she started young enough to manage such a goodly crowd.)

Incidentally, I had the opportunity to examine fairly thoroughly the Chaplin marriage when, at one time, they lived directly behind us in the old Chaplin mansion. There they had school rooms for the children and a large staff of nursery maids. Chaplin had everything done the way he wanted it. He was quite a wild tennis player (then in his late sixties) and Oona would organize large tea parties out by the tennis court where she would sit with the guests and watch all the games. The children were kept away, being entertained elsewhere by the nurses—Oona organized that for him too. Certainly, she didn't inflict her family on their father. He seemed to be a fond parent, always chucking somebody under the chin or stroking a small head of hair, but such fondling wasn't very time consuming.

In the case of the Chaplins, the children seemed to be the only losers. Although Geraldine has been very successful for so young an actress, I would judge she is not a very soft or a very loving girl. The son, Michael, of course has written his own story and exposed much more than I've gone into. Vari-

21

ous other children of the Chaplins also bespeak a selfish father.

Yet, it didn't make a bad marriage for a young woman. She had her family life, her babies, and apparently because she was willing to dance attendance on the real star of the family, Charles Chaplin, she was able to make a fairly nice existence for herself. Probably it was Oona's youth that gave her the necessary adaptability to Chaplin's ways, his moods and his pomposities (of which he had plenty). And it gave her the tolerance to accept his domination and whatever strange habits he may have had. Because she was not set in her own ways she was able to get along with him. As a result, I think she should receive the full credit for making that marriage go.

Possibly the same thing applies to *any* marriage of an older man to a young girl. *She* makes the adaptation. He doesn't. By the time he's in his forties or fifties, he couldn't possibly try to be the fellow some young girl dreams about. She must try to be the woman *he* dreams about.

Unlike Chaplin, many elderly men who marry a younger woman wanting to raise a family are not able to do so single-handedly, so to speak. Since these men don't want to go into the streets looking for a fellow to help them out, they turn to artificial insemination. This method has been used by at least two Hollywood celebrities, without damage to their marriages—although it does seem a rather sordid way for a young woman to become a mother for the first time.

In both of these instances, the father, until that time, had been unable to produce a child after trying with several wives—and then in his sixties, a young wife had given him an artificially inseminated baby. But what difference did that make? The men had become very proud parents because of the special effort involved. Most people become parents by sheer accident, due to not looking where they were going, but for these men it was a sought-after event. No doubt it gives a great boot to an older man to find himself the father of a young child.

My own father, at the age of seventy and his wife, my stepmother, adopted a little two-year-old Greek girl who certainly added a great deal of pleasure to their lives. My father has enjoyed this child immensely because for the first time in his life he has some leisure. That just wasn't the case when he was young and had his own children. In fact, I often think the pleasures of parenthood should be saved for the old. It's rather a shame we always get babies when we least can afford them and have the least time to spend with them.

So the older-man-younger-woman marriage would seem to be a good idea. In return for a few years of happiness and love, the man treats the woman tenderly and patiently. Surely there are plenty of cases to prove the practicality of this situation. Just to mention a few in Hollywood: Bing Crosby and Kathy with at least a twenty to thirty year age difference. Howard Hughes and Jean Peters. Harry Karl and Debbie Reynolds. Other famous older husbands are John Wayne, Robert Taylor and Henry Fonda—all doing quite well.

In the case of Glenn Ford and young Kathy Hayes, it's amazing to note that Glenn formerly was at the other end of a similar type marriage, having been some years the junior of his first wife, Eleanor Powell. Now he's trying it the other way around.

Which brings us to the opposite side of the tree—the older ladies who marry younger boys. For instance, Sybil Burton and Jordan Christopher with an age difference of between twelve and fifteen years. Or the extreme case of the dress designer Marusia who married a boy of about twenty-three. (Her age is unknown but certainly more than twice his.)

There's about eight to ten years difference between the famous stage performers, Lynn Fontanne and Alfred Lunt. With nature taking a hand, Alfred has been ailing for years while she has gone blooming on. Collette, who was considered to be the greatest writer in our century on the subject of love, devoted herself to the relationship between older women and younger men, and in fact herself was married for the third time, when in her late fifties, to a man fifteen years younger. When she died at eighty, he still was at her side, apparently contented all those years.

In Hollywood, there are Norma Shearer and Marty Arrouge who have been married for about twenty years. The age difference probably is considerable, but to this day they eat dinner alone together by choice in various restaurants, always chatting happily.

The greatest example in our town is the long-lasting marriage of Mary Pickford and Buddy Rogers. He was an extremely good-looking young man, at least twenty years younger than she and on the brink of a very good career. He gave it up to marry Mary Pickford and I have never heard any scandal about either of them.

There are many other examples that can't be mentioned for special reasons. The women are considerably older than the men but their marriages are continuing because the men aren't men at all. Each of them is covering his homosexuality by being a gracious escort to an older woman who's grateful for his company, makes no physical demands on him and allows him his way with the fellows.

Such examples abound in the interior decorating business and in the movie industry. At one time it was said there were no homosexual males successful on the screen. Nobody could claim that has been true in the last few years. Some of the most popular male performers in films are not in the least bit masculine. No names, please.

Aside from these odd cases though, the older-woman younger-man marriage too is a practical idea for both parties. For the woman, first of all, there is the advantage of having a young man who of course is as pliable as a young woman. He is willing to learn and adjust and see things her way. He has none of the pig-headedness that a grown up older man has; he has none of the physical problems an older man is sure to have developed; he is not tired of an evening; he's not even tired of a morning. If it's a question of having a little physical love, he is physically able at all times, usually rather willing and sometimes very eager.

This is a different story from having to entice and coax and encourage one who has waning powers. Men suffer very much with the loss of virility. No matter how they may lie about it, this is very obvious to one who has ever been around. There are men who boast loudly they are just as good as they ever were but it just ain't true. Unless they are master men who do nothing else, there are few men who can come up to scratch in their forties as they did in their twenties.

Many older men have developed certain deviations. They need to take Sodium Amytal or other stimulating drugs to get them going. Or they need to see something hideous on the ceiling, or wall, or in pictures. Or they have to go watch two bulls kill each other. Or they need to use a whip. They have all sorts of peculiar methods that might get them going—or might not.

These older men rarely respond automatically just to the sight of a woman they like. In fact, they hardly ever *like* a woman that much because they're full of caginess. *Is she after the dinners? Is she hoping to marry me? What does she want of me?* Young men don't ask themselves such questions. *Can I get her or can't I?* That's the entire issue to a young man. If she is available and if she'll let him, he'll be there on time and he'll be at her very fast, regardless of dainty introductions.

Naturally, this is quite refreshing to the older woman who's been used to a slowing-down type of man who is full of apologies: "Sorry, I must have drunk too much." "Sorry, I forgot to take my vitamins." "Sorry, I was overtired." If she's a normal woman, she's going to be pretty fed up with that. There's nothing more boring than having to work very hard to stir a man to action when sheer vanity demands that the very sight of her should be sufficient to drive him out of his mind.

After all, a bull or a tomcat doesn't need to be

27

danced around a few hundred times. They simply have to know the animal of the opposite sex is there. Women expect the same. It's flattering to assume that a man looks across a crowded room, sees you and is ready for you then and there. But this doesn't happen with older men. First of all, they can't even *see* you across a crowded room. And they're certainly not ready.

So, from a physical point of view, the woman who has passed the fear of becoming pregnant every twenty minutes, who now has some spare time on her hands and a little savoir faire, appreciates a young eager lover more than a tired disagreeable one. (Also one with a backache.) Aside from that, the younger man provides an older woman with instant happy companionship instead of complaining and whizzling and grizzling companionship. Usually, he is full of hope rather than despair. He wants to hear her every thought and he wants to share his. Older men are very unchatty as a rule and they certainly don't want to hear a lot of guff from some older woman.

The young man gets a fairly good deal of such a marriage too. Usually, he doesn't want to be getting somebody pregnant every time he turns around. He doesn't want to take on any responsibilities if he can avoid them. He wants to have an active love life and he certainly can get it from an older woman. He also wants to have an active daytime existence. He wants to go out and about, he wants to dance and play, he wants to talk and think, and he wants to read aloud.

A young woman is apt to say, "Oh, I can't be bothered now because I'll be doing my eyebrows for the next two hours." Young girls often are very inconsiderate of young men. They resent their need for so much encouragement and so much entertainment.

There are some quite obvious emotional reasons as well as obvious physical reasons in favor of this kind of marriage. An older woman can give a great deal of comfort to a younger man when he's wondering if he's ever going to make anything of himself. And she isn't going to ask him for much if she's lucky enough to get a younger man. She's willing to forego such mundane things as support. For one thing, she won't be there long enough to need much.

A young man, out in the world, wants to be taken care of to some extent. The older woman satisfies some of his need to be mothered and loved and fussed over. Naturally, then he is delighted with her company, enchanted to be admired by someone who wishes to teach him all the things of life she knows.

He also gets a certain amount of help with choosing his shirts and any other little necessities of life. Best of all, she can't make demands. They say older women are great lovers because they're so grateful. Appreciation for what you're getting and also for what you're not getting, only comes with age. The aggravation of having a husband who refuses to mow the lawn can never come with the older woman married to a young man. After all, he's her lover and she wouldn't dream of asking him to do anything so dreary as mowing the lawn. He's a bit of luck. You don't turn him to other useful purposes. Let him rest. You may be needing him later.

In my opinion, another good reason for the young-old marriage is the fact that there is far less lying between people of vastly different age groups. Those in the same age bracket have already decided to keep their innermost selves shut off. But when dealing with an older woman, a young man will not hold back. He'll tell the truth all the way because he wants to hear reactions.

An older woman will tell a young man things she wouldn't tell anyone else because she feels she's handing on the sum total of her experiences. And a young girl will tell her hopes and dreams to an older man because in a way he's daddy—a daddy she never really had. Her own father, I'm sure, wouldn't have had time to listen and probably she wouldn't have felt free to tell him either. And an older man may confide his hopes and dreams to a young girl because they won't seem as absurd and silly as they might to somebody his own age.

A well-known lawyer once said to me, "Older people who marry younger people are simply buying a little happiness for a short time." Nothing in life is permanent—even May-December marriages. One or the other may die at any time—or one or the other may split out and find another mate. But, for whatever time it lasts, it sounds to me like much more fun, much more excitement and much more satisfaction than is offered by the conventional age-alike type of marriage considered normal today.

3 { MARRIAGE IS BEDLAM

Basically, sex is quite a peculiar and very individual thing. Nobody really knows what goes on behind the bedroom door in someone else's home. For instance, I have a friend who is married to a movie star and has been unfaithful to him on and off for a number of years. She tells me, instead of being jealous, the only time her husband shows any real interest in her is when he suspects she is involved with another man. As soon as he notices she is staying out for hours in the afternoon and nipping off for a weekend whenever possible, she can't get through the front door before he sweeps her up to bed. However, once he realizes she has dumped the other man and is behaving in a sedate, wifely manner, his interest flags and he stops leaping at her at every turn or trying to get her into bed. He never accuses her or does anything about the situation because obviously he is stimulated only by the thought of his wife being desirable to some other man.

I have another friend, who, in almost twenty years of marriage has been paid for every sexual contact with her husband. The fee varies according to the circumstances. If he wants her to leave the children and go away with him for a few days, she may demand as much as three hundred dollars, and though he can well afford the price, he likes to bargain with her, saying, "Come on, make it two hundred and fifty." Sometimes, just for the spur of the moment divertissement, she will ask, "How much cash do you have on you?" He'll empty his pockets of twenty or thirty dollars, and she'll say, "Sorry. Not enough." He'll plead, "Will you take a check?" "No, this is strictly cash and carry." So it might very well turn out to be a case of Not tonight, Josephine. Some people might consider such an approach crass and unromantic. But for this couple, it lends a spice to the entire act.

Psychologists will tell you most people have fetishes of some sort, no matter how weirdly small. Very often a person is stuck on the thing that first alerted him to sex. That's why some men are aroused by the sight of an ankle even though ankles are pretty commonplace today. With other people the fire can be kindled only by something a little higher up the line. The very sophisticated person always carries his fetish with him in his mind's eye and, therefore, can operate effectively with almost anybody who isn't repulsive, provided nothing revolting is said or done. Naturally, this can be a boon to marriage especially after the first exciting years. And let's face it, those first exciting years (or sometimes only months or weeks) do fly by.

There's a theory that, with a good sex adjustment in marriage, almost anything else can go by the boards. The couple involved will get along nicely despite any other problems—and to some extent that must be true. If a man's wife really attracts him he'll forgive her many other faults, and certainly most women can't achieve a good sexual relationship with a man unless they also have found other worthwhile traits in him. Therefore, it's difficult to imagine a marriage where the sex life is working wonderfully well and the rest of it isn't working pretty well too. Undoubtedly it's easier to make up a quarrel when sexually compatible. Often lovers have quarrels only for the pleasure of making up. The quarrel, in these cases, is not caused by a basic hatred of each other but by a deep fascination with the game of fighting and then hopping into bed. An example of this is the splendidly tough actor who fought violently, privately and publicly, with his wife but never had a thought of breaking up the marriage until many years later when the old thrill was gone—and a new thrill had come along.

At any rate sex should play a major role in the early stages of marriage. If sex falls by the wayside too soon, the marriage tends to disintegrate at the same time—probably because most men are always hunters to a certain extent and women become disappointed to find themselves not so much desired as previously. In marriage for the long pull though, sex can't play the biggest part. In the natural course of intimacy, sleeping in the same room is bound to become less interesting. In fact, anything in surplus grows less exciting to us—only the little tidbits that are handed out tantalizingly continue to intrigue us. Most women feel that sex in marriage is grossly over-rated. A wife usually has no difficulty in keeping up with her husband if he's attractive to her and has any real sex interest. But most men, after a certain period of marriage, gradually lose their original zest for making love, probably because they're worn out with just keeping up with their work and other everyday activities. Actually this is perfectly natural if you consider that nature obviously intended man to get sexy only for a short interval every ten months. Once he had made his wife pregnant there was no point, whatever, in repeating the act. After that he could wait until six weeks after childbirth and then do it once more. That's the normal procedure for animals in their own time cycle—only men try to beat a dead horse into an activity for regular use, and most of them don't entirely succeed.

I believe any man can do an occasional one-night stand with a new partner because the very novelty brings excitement. If he's sitting in front of a TV set, slogging away at a beer with someone he knows very well and then rolls sleepy-eyed into bed, he doesn't feel especially sexy. But if he's been hot-footing it around town, trying to get in at the back door somewhere, running the great risk that a husband or father will hear him creeping up the stairs, he's breathlessly impassioned. This experience may seem to him like the Fountain of Youth, but twenty minutes later when he finds it in his own bed, he probably couldn't perform for the life of him. These facts of life are particularly sad for the people who marry only for physical reasons, needing a bed companion at all costs. In due time the ecstacy ends in a horrible letdown and the agony sets in. If there are children in the picture, these people may stay together, being unfaithful whenever an opportunity arises. It's even more tragic for those who are drawn together by a powerful sex attraction but really dislike each other. Usually, each will continue punishing the other until the lure of sex has disappeared entirely and only the punishment is left.

Some people are aware of the fleeting quality of sex and can't be enticed into a marriage based on this one attraction. A prominent television personality told me that, although he had been very fond of a blonde glamour figure, he had turned down her proposal of marriage, saying, "We never can get married, darling, because all we have together is being in bed. When we're not in bed, there's nothing to talk about."

Certain men claim sex gives them drive. I don't believe this. I think the sexy man hangs around picking up girls while the un-sexy one gets on with the business of using his drive productively elsewhere. The same applies to women. Those who have lots of children aren't necessarily sexy, nor those with no children, un-sexy. The enjoyment of sex is simply nature's trick to force us into reproducing, and the difference between man and animal is man's need for companionship, his yearning to get rid of his loneliness by establishing communication. Sex really is only a temporary form of communication; it leads nowhere and it's over when it's over—especially for a man. He can lay everything from a pumpkin to a pillow and walk away from it. Similarly any woman who's been casual in her relationships also knows she can walk away from it. Ask her to make a list of past lovers and she's likely to leave out several. Remind her, "Didn't you once say you had an affair with—?" And she'll answer, "Really? Did I? Yes, on second thought, maybe I did." It had been completely forgotten, proof of its unimportance in her life.

Also, sex plays a very small role in marriage, timewise. Even Zsa Zsa once said of Rubirosa, "He may be the best lover in the world but what do you do the other twenty-two hours of the day?" You can make love only so long and then you have the rest of your life to kill. When the only interest you share with another person is in physical accomplishment, it can get pretty grim yawning your way through the day, waiting for night to fall. And so eventually the relationship must end completely. Everyone knows of some young passionate marriage entered into by a couple of kids so wildly in love they couldn't come in out of the car all night, then six months after they were married, it was over, finished and goodby forever.

Therefore, a good marriage really isn't a sex relationship. If you asked a truly happily married individual, "If one or the other of you were paralyzed and you never could have sex relations again, would your marriage break up?"—the answer would be, "Not at all." The marriage would go on because if the other things in it were good, they'd be far more important, whereas if sex were all, there'd be no point in staying on with a cripple. Many a

man has married an invalid and been very happy
with her—and time and time again, women have
stuck to men who were completely sexless and also
have been very happy. An example of this was the
last marriage of a famous—the most famous of
them all—film star who reportedly was completely
incapable in any way whatsoever with a woman and
always had been. When one of his exwives was asked,
"How could you possibly have divorced him—the
most beautiful man in the world?" she is quoted as
having replied, "I kept thinking, *If he comes into my
room once more carrying that little black bag, I think
I'll scream!*" (The little black bag contained a vi-
brator. That was the actor's only offering in a sex
life.) But the real problem in that marriage was
their incompatibility of tastes and outlook on life.
His next marriage to a more suitable, congenial
woman was completely satisfactory to both parties,
despite his physical impotence.

It's the mental attitude that really counts in marriage—the ability to talk to each other and to feel
for each other. Speaking from a woman's point of
view, there are many men who are attractive sexually but they don't touch your heart at all. You're
not worried about their going on plane trips. If you
hear they have pneumonia, all you think is, *Oh goodness, I do hope he'll be all right in time for the party
next Saturday.* You don't really care. Another man,

40

not so attractive, may come along and your sympathy is aroused. You're concerned about his driving too fast, smoking too much and forgetting his raincoat on wet days. This isn't a physical emotion so evidently love has little to do with sex.

⌈I think it's unfortunate that magazines and films promote the illusion that passionate kisses mean everlasting love and a great night in bed is going to result in an eighty year marriage during which every thought will be communicated to the mate. In point of fact, communication of thoughts is a very subtle procedure, depending on the same wave length operating between people and really has nothing to do with a physical relationship. In my opinion, there are an enormous number of marriages where sex doesn't enter at all. With people who have been joined together for as long as forty or fifty years, probably the last thirty years have been "sans" sex.⌋

Nevertheless, there is a time in people's lives when sex does become important. During the menopause and man's change of life, both men and women become desperate to prove something. They feel life is slipping by—there's no fun in it—and they need the lift of being "in love." The in-love feeling is a kind of unreal and emotional skit, a jump over the moon that usually requires some sort of sex impulse to get it going. But even this need is

41

by-passed by the many people who have fallen wildly in love from afar. In fact, the whole phenomena of loving film performers is in this vein. It's the thrill of being devoted to Elvis Presley without ever seeing him personally, without ever taking the risk of getting to know him and learning he is just like anybody else. (Of course, he isn't—he's lovely!)

The ideal of marriage has been built up for centuries. Universally people have dreamed that love would be eternal. By this reasoning, since marriage is the ideal of adult love, then sex must go with adult love, must be one and the same thing. Many of us know that love and sex do not necesarily tie in together at all, nor do marriage and sex, but we're fighting a losing battle. Considering that our entire culture has been built on such a false notion, how can we explain away the fallacy to our own children?

4 { MARRIAGE IS A DELICATE CONDITION

Somebody once said a love affair lasts five years as a rule and only the very lucky affairs last longer. The same goes for marriage, unless something has been added to it. Some marriages build into such great companionships that there's enough there, and some build into such dependencies that there's no escaping them. The majority of marriages suffer a great deal with the passing of time and a great deal of communication slips out of them unless there are children. Children do add to a family life because without them you have no family.

Most everybody wants to have children sooner or later but they usually put it off if they can. They think it's an inconvenient time or it's too expensive or they'd rather take a trip or vacation. Actually there is no convenient time to have children. In my opinion, it's foolish to put off too long having them and, at the same time, it's foolish to have them the first year because the man and wife do not have a chance to get to know each other before they're faced with some very large problems. Too many children, too soon, bring on a tired wife and an overextended husband, from the financial point of view.

Even the good father who is quite happily settled at home finds the kids more than tough to take most of the time. He does not have a strong maternal instinct and a paternal instinct doesn't mean a thing. There are moments in most men's lives when they feel proud to see their son or daughter graduating with honors or bringing great glory to the firm. But as for their sticky little hands, and those dirty diapers, and those slight upchucks at the dining room table, and the failure to get to the toilet at the right moment—somehow or other leave most fathers cold. Mother, naturally, is a little more sympathetic when she finds her favorite son is pilfering out of her handbag or has secreted a frog in her bed. She realizes that boys will be boys but it's hard to make a man realize it. Since he's no longer a boy himself, he doesn't see why anybody else should be allowed the privilege.

Seriously speaking though, I think parenthood is a highly over-rated pastime. It's true that being a mother satisfies a biological urge in a woman (usually at a time when she hoped it wasn't going to be satisfied), but it also takes away her right to be herself. I think only a very mature woman can recognize the good of motherhood. Any woman can recognize its obvious fun, like when she brings home that teeny-weeny baby from the hospital and everybody admires it for the first six days. But after that, exhaustion sets in and very few mothers can say they really loved having their babies and keeping them for the first year or so when they were completely helpless. The sight of a young and frantic mother can be seen any time in any supermarket.

I think it would be fair to say that many marriages are broken up by the arrival of a first child, although the actual split may not show up until many years later. A couple may have been divinely close right up until the advent of the little dictator, and though the man may try to stick it out, hoping that sooner or later things will get to be good again between them—and they may stick it out until there are one or two or three children—eventually the split will show. It's hard to prove that it definitely dates from the arrival of the first child, but often it does. A man may resent his wife's servitude to the child and the lack of privacy that having a family brings and many a wife becomes "too tired" after the birth of a baby.

It's usually thought that children are capable of

making a marriage have purpose, keeping it in good condition, giving mutual interest and, of course, having children is basically the purpose of marriage anyway. Some people are so misinformed as to figure if their marriage is about to go on the rocks, the arrival of a new baby may help to prevent it. I think nothing could be further from the truth. Most people would like to find a mother or a father figure who would understand them as perfectly as their own mother and father didn't. Usually when they marry they are seeking sexual satisfaction but at the same time, on the side—and a very large side it is since there's only a certain amount of time that can be devoted to sex even in the most active partners, they are attempting to utilize the partner as a mother or father substitute, not just any old mother and father but a satisfactory one. So what happens? Expecting to find themselves marvelously parented, they become parents instead.

Many marriages which break up in Hollywood where the announcements are fairly well covered include couples with a one-year-old or two-year-old child. Whether the child definitely was responsible for splitting up the couple, who can say? But you can bet it didn't help. The marriage of Julie Andrews hasn't seemed too healthy since the birth of her daughter. Sandra Dee and Bobby Darrin split while fairly new parents. Samantha Eggers' first marriage ended soon after she had a child. Some years ago the marriage of director Leslie Stevens and actress Kate Manx fell apart while they had very young children and subsequently she committed suicide. Even if they didn't cause the break-up, the children in these cases certainly didn't weld any of these marriages together.

Having children is one thing and having a lover is another. And even being extremely companionable, it just isn't necessarily so that a family life leads to bigger and better understandings. I might quote that my own parents were divorced after the arrival of their sixth child when my mother was only about 33 and my father, 36. They'd been married ten years, just long enough to get in that family, and I don't think they've ever spoken since.

I think often romance makes a grand exit after the pregnant lady looms on the scene. Most men may feel they have a sentimental attachment to that large stomach but in point of fact, they're only paying lip service to the training they're had in momism. Very few men have the perversion of being grotesquely attracted to pregnant ladies. The average man sees the unpregnant woman as a sexual symbol but there's really no quicker way to drive him out of your bed and into someone else's than to be permanently with child. Little cryings and wailings in the night and little teething problems are a great big, crashing bore to a fellow who has to go to work in the morning. Not that they aren't quite a bore to the average mother but she is prepared for such things, expects them and has the comfort of knowing that the baby really does enjoy being in her arms. This somehow is a sop to woman's wounded vanity and makes her feel she's needed, at least by the miniature creature. I think it would be smart for people to indulge in a little introspection before they get involved in any of this stuff, asking themselves why they want a family in the first place and what they expect it will do to and for them. If it's love and romance they want, of course they should stay as far away from having children as they can.

There was a move recently toward fathers being present at the birth of their young, with naturally some disastrous effects. Many a man will faint just watching you cut up the dog's meat, let alone seeing his wife on an operating table giving birth to his young. Soon after I had my first child, a girl I knew confided in me that her husband was going to be present during the complete birth of their first child. She was one of those angelic, blonde creatures who fluffed through her pregnancy in white floating robes, and he was a very dashing looking director. I didn't know her very well but I begged her not to let him be in at the kill, so to speak. I tried to explain in as couth terms as I could find how unromantic she would be looking at that particular time and how difficult it is for a man to adjust himself to the sight of that rather large and unwieldy stomach painted with various strange shades of antiseptic—sometimes blue and sometimes orange—legs in stirrups, spotlights all over, a masked cast of nurses and doctors, knives and scalpels flying, and blood splashing all over the white uniforms. If the wife is lucky and unconscious, at least she isn't aware of any grunts and groans and moans and even, heaven forbid, upchuckery that she may go in for. And if she is conscious, she may be a bit put out to find she has become a snarling, howling mass of animal. No matter how briefly the whole thing goes or how good your doctor is, there are bound to be a few slightly untidy, to say the least, moments that you might be grateful afterward that your lover had not seen. Needless to say, my friend did not pay any attention to my advice and two babies later, they were divorced. I notice that his new wife has been clever enough to have no children.

I don't think it should be considered unrealistic and mean of men to find themselves slightly put off a woman whom they've seen in the extremes of childbirth. After all, no animal comes out and exhibits itself in so forthright a fashion. Most discreet animals snuggle under the straw or the hedge and give birth in the dark of the night. Only *we* put a spotlight on it all and play for the audience, and I think a man is entitled to his illusions. Nature never intended him to have anything to do with birth. His whole job was over ten months before and barring a few kind remarks and a nice bunch of flowers, that's where he belongs—out. Woman's work is never done as they say—and quite obviously when it comes to childbirth, it can only be *her* work, aided and abetted by a few sadistic doctors.

To add insult to injury, many fathers suffer the pangs of neglect when she comes home from the hospital with that brand new item which she feels really is all her own—and so it is. Once upon a time the father was the baby boy at home and now look who's getting all the attention! It isn't easy for a man, especially a young one. Even some of the older fathers haven't made out so well. Some people say an older man is more able to cope with the difficulties of raising a family. However, I would question the validity of that. Older men are more irritable, more set in their ways, less resilient. If they got by without having a family, they've no doubt been spoiled rotten, and they're not about to change that if they can help it. Theoretically a man who has remained childless until he's forty may feel, *Wouldn't it be wonderful if I had a son to carry on my name—John Smith, Esquire!* But when the practical aspect of the whole thing bursts upon him and he realizes that when his son is 15, he'll be 55, and when his son is 21, he'll be 60, he has to admit it will look a bit absurd and perhaps he won't have the patience that is needed to develop a good friendly relationship with an unwilling relation.

A man is fairly gratified by teen-age children provided they pay some lip service to his authority, but very few men really can enjoy those first few months while the little thing crosses its eyes, burps, spits up and does a few other things that are unmentionable, usually all at the same time. The wife who really loves her love affair would be wise to put off having her children until the love affair is on the wane and then, since it's going anyhow, she can trim it off fast by developing a family. In this way, she'll have young children to see her through her divorce and guarantee her some sort of an income (if the court can find him) and some company to occupy her until she finds another man.

Some people stay together when they have children only because it's too expensive to part. And there are very few parents who ever would be able to say openly that they wish they'd never had their children, although I'll bet there are quite a few who wonder in the dark of the night, *Oh, why did I ever do it?* You can't help loving them when they're there but they definitely are a distraction and kind of put you off concentrating on yourself who, after all, was your favorite person in the first place.

51

5 { MARRIAGE IS
FOR BOSOM PALS

Once on an airplane coming back from New York I
was sitting beside Tony Martin, the long-time husband of Cyd Charise. We were discussing my im-
pending divorce and he said, "Well, all I can advise
you is—if you're ever going to marry again—be
sure you marry a friend." I'm quite certain that of all
the advice I've ever received, that probably was the
very best. I don't suppose I'm the kind of person
who can take advice but that stuck in my mind and
the more I thought about marriage and other people's marriages, the more I looked to see if there
was any possibility that those two people might be
friends.

Every so often you see what seems to be a good
marriage. Let me mention a couple I've seen over

the years. Salvador Dali and his wife—I remember once meeting her at the home of another friendly married couple, Jean Renoir and his wife, Dido. Mrs. Dali was chatting about my—at that time— brand new baby Portland, and I asked her if she had any children and she said, "Oh no, why would I have any children? I have him," indicating Dali. I thought, *what a waste of time, making a baby out of a man.* (Although we all do that.) But afterward, looking back on the whole thing, I realized that a woman who wants such a marriage had better not have children. If she has a good friend in a husband and can be a good friend to him, she probably has the best companionship life can offer.

It isn't everyone who is able to marry for friendship. Most people marry for a variety of economic and sexual reasons, most of which fall apart when they get to know each other better. If they set out looking for a good buddy, they'd probably be more on the right track. It's an unlikely thing that a person will feel the same toward someone he meets when in his teens or early twenties as he will toward someone he meets when he's forty or fifty and marries at that time. To make a long-time life-long marriage there must be an enormous amount of mutual understanding, mutual consideration and mutual dreams plus a willingness to meet in the middle.

Quite late in my life, my father wrote to me and

said, "It's not enough that this man loves you. What do you have in common?" I felt like writing back and saying, "The only thing in the world that matters is that he loves me," but on second thought I knew that a mutual love of me could end in the same sort of dust that comes to most marriages. If we had nothing else to talk about, nothing to do together and no pipe-dreams to share, there could be nothing long-term in it. Even sharing a family does not necessarily add to your happiness together —sometimes quite the reverse. The only thing you need to share is each other—and to be able to do that successfully for many years takes quite a bit of friendliness.]

I think that romance, much as I love it, is probably a very false step in the direction of starting a long-time relationship. I'm not sure that romance and marriage are at all compatible. It only works out if the right two people get that romantic glow and also find they have enough of other things they can share—a liking for the same kind of pastimes and the same interest in civic affairs and politics. Oh, there are some people who say they and their mate have voted differently for years and in spite of their violent political differences, they still are the best of friends. I, personally, couldn't bear the idea of having a bitter fight with the man I love because he's of one political party and I another. It would seem to me the least he could do would be to turn my way or, if I really loved him, I'm sure I would see it his way.

I don't think differences of opinion necessarily mean one can't get along with a person, but it would seem that people who are divinely suited to each other probably think alike. I know that in the good years of my marriage to James Mason, we thought so much alike, we could have told each other exactly what we would think of a play or a book or a film. We would know each other's reaction and be completely correct on it and mostly in agreement. That changed as we grew older but it lasted for at least ten years and I would think that is the right foundation for a friendship in marriage. You must agree on practically everything. You must understand about your in-laws; you must see eye-to-eye on family life; you must both like animals to the same degree or dislike them.

I always think a marriage is doomed when a man decides he's not going to have any pets in the house though his wife has always had a Persian cat. She may put up with it for the first few years and then she'll think of all the joys he's taken from her. Similarly, a man who hates dancing and a woman who loves it; a man who's mad about baseball and a woman who detests it. They may manage while the romance is hot and the sex symbol of their lives is at high mast but when those attractions fly away, they will find themselves pretty damned bored with each other and with many years to kill. I think the death of most marriages probably is the boredom, and the best way to avoid boredom is to have mutual understanding and mutual interests. There are many things that can come between you, like other people, children, love affairs, money troubles, health problems, jealousy—there are a thousand things waiting around the corner in every romance to tear it to shreds. So it takes a lively-minded man and a lively-minded woman, both of whom are intent on making their friendship or marriage work, to really succeed at it.

Somebody once told me he thought it was disastrous for couples to work together because inevitably a competitive attitude came into it and if the wife surpassed the husband, the marriage was more threatened than it would have been had she been working in somebody else's office. I don't go along with that. I think a marriage that is threatened by that sort of thing was threatened in the first place. However, my own opinion is that the woman should be subservient to the man for her own happiness and comfort and for the good of his ego. If one of the parties is to be superior in power and in decision-making, it would be a good idea if that person was the man. If it happens to be the woman, it takes a special man to be able to be as satisfied as if he was the ruler of the roost. If he is that kind of a man and is prepared from the very beginning to not try to usurp his wife's position but instead be an aid to her, then he certainly can be just as happy as any other man.

I think if a husband and wife can work, together with the same aims, obviously they are one up on the game. Ancient families always worked within the family and the old Italian system of putting mama behind the cash register while papa did the cooking or the serving in the restaurant, has worked out for generations. They are equally interested in the success of their business whereas the wife in the average American home is fed up with hearing about his business because she doesn't share it. All she shares are the proceeds and that isn't enough. It would be much better for her to be sharing some of the labor, some of the worry and some of the anxieties and having something to discuss when they're alone together. It might be argued that a couple in business together might have all their spare time taken up with discussing business. Well, it's better to discuss business than not to discuss anything, which is one of the complaints of the average wife. He comes home; he says, "Hello," and "What's for dinner?"; he picks up the paper and turns on the TV and that's it. They've nothing to discuss because they have nothing of mutual interest. He doesn't care about her marketing problems; he isn't interested in what happened to the disposal and he's not all that crazy about hearing the news of the children. If they were sharing the worries about his business, she at least would be a part of his life, the part that really takes up most of his time. So if one is to try and design the ideal marriage, I would say it definitely is an advantage to work together if not in business, at some hobby like photography or painting.

In show business, there are many happy couples who work together. The Fredric March-Florence Eldridge marriage has lasted for goodness knows how long, through many a thick and thin. He was—and still is—one of the most attractive men in the movies and she was a very big star when they met. They linked up and have managed to make a go of it, apparently extremely happily. Lunt and Fontaine of course is a most notable example. Katherine Cornell and Guthrie McClintock worked together considerably and their marriage ended only with his death after about thirty years of togetherness. Helen Hayes and Charles MacArthur had a similarly happy marriage of about thirty years of trial and error. Then there are Ruth Gordon and Garson Kanin who write together and work together as much as they can, very successfully. Also, Edye

Gorme and Steve Lawrence and Peter Lind Hayes and Mary Healy, also Hume Cronyn and Jessica Tandy. It's easy to pick out the famous ones because one hears of them. It's not so easy to find the infamous ones, no insult intended.

Of course working together, though it may help, is no guarantee of a long happy friendship in marriage. Examples of cases where it didn't work are: Lawrence Olivier and Vivien Leigh, Lucy and Desi, and very recently, Sheila and Gordon MacCrea. Even in politics where there are many examples of people who have long, companionable marriages, there are exceptions to the rule—Governor Rockefeller being a classic example. But most political figures, knowing on which side their votes are buttered, make their marriages work and seem like beautiful friendships even if they really aren't. A few happily married public figures who were at one time entertainers are Ronald Reagan, once married to actress Jane Wyman, now quite contented for a long while with the former Nancy Davis (also a sometime actress.) George Murphy has had only one marriage and a good one. Both of these seem to be fine friendships too.

Perhaps it's only a wild hope that two people of opposite sex can find a complete, understanding friendship with equal respect to each partner. It certainly must be a rare circumstance, considering the number of marriages that wind up in the divorce courts, and yet if it can bring to two people a really long and satisfying relationship, it's well worth looking for and clutching tightly forever when once it's found.

6 { MARRIAGE IS A STATE OF HATE

I have a theory that biological facts are our worst enemies. For instance, we all know it is natural for the male to be somewhat of a tom-cat, depending on his energy and the amount of work he has to put in elsewhere. The female, on the other hand, was made to build nests and lay eggs in them, so to speak. Now, most of one's grown-up life, the female is making desperate efforts to avoid getting into a situation where she will be laying an egg. She has various mechanical devices and various unpleasant squashy kinds of jelly, etc., which may keep her out of that situation and she can, if she is strong-minded or religious enough, hold the man at arm's length until she's ready to have a family. (But we aren't going to even consider that method because it's a very unreliable one and one which few normal human beings want to indulge in if they can avoid it.) Nowadays the pill is the star. It not only fills out one's wrinkles, spurns menopause for quite some time, inflates one's bosoms and strengthens one's bones, but it also prevents unwanted pregnancies. And most pregnancies are unwanted at the time.

I think the proper explanation for premenstrual tension is that most women, in spite of their frantic efforts to avoid pregnancy, cannot help but resent a man who's allowed them to succeed in avoiding it. It's all very well intellectually facing the fact that we cannot afford a baby right now, especially if we aren't married, but a woman's body doesn't recognize any of those financial facts. Her body prepares itself for a pregnancy. If she happens to be lucky enough to have found a man, her body assumes that he's going to make a success of this natural biological urge. Her body is ignorant of the fact that she's used mechanical devices or taken a pill. Her body tells her that this man is a total failure since the month has come around again and she's not pregnant. So she begins to snap and snarl at him, attack him, criticize him, find his legs too hairy, his chin too underslung, his voice too weak and his pocketbook not fat enough.

Most of us spend our entire lives fighting against our own natures. It is normal for a woman to be pacified by pregnancy. Most healthy women find themselves in the bloom of their health, at least by the fourth month. They feel gorgeous; they look better than they've ever looked (except of course around the middle) and their skins improve, their temperaments improve, and a fat and sassy attitude comes over them. (It becomes a very diffcrent thing when they start changing diapers however.) Therefore, I consider any woman who is having a normal four-weekly cycle a frustrated woman, since nature obviously intended us to have a couple of those and then a ten-month out of season, but we stopped all that.

I don't know if anybody has noticed but women who have had an exhorbitant number of children— Maureen O'Sullivan, (seven, I believe); Mrs. Bobby Kennedy, (ten or twelve, I'm not sure of the latest count); Oona O'Neill Chaplin, (seven or nine); Jeanne Crain, (five or six); Ann Blythe, (about six);—all look extremely young, are extremely energetic and have kept their figures. It's we who had only two children who have grown fat eating too much with energy to spare as each month rolls around and no pregnancy has resulted from those passionate love affairs. One can't help but wonder—have these other women so much better men? This is a biological wonder and not an intellectual one. You can look at their men and answer that question for yourself. So, no doubt, your body is sneering heartily at your mate for having failed to produce the large number of children that your egg-making system had lined up for you.

Over a period of years, this biological hatred builds up into a fantastic elemental loathing and the man never quite understands why he's so put upon and so nagged at, but the childless woman will invariably take it out on him in one way or another, never knowing what it is that she basically despises about him. She'll often tell her friends, "He's really very good to me. He's sweet, he's companionable, he's very kind, and he's not too bad a dancer, but nevertheless he gets on my nerves." Why? Because nature already had decided what he was supposed to be doing for her and nature knows he has failed and in the determination to continue the race, nature's method would be to get rid of that man as quickly as possible and get a more successful one in. But we spend most of our lives working against our natures anyhow and it never would occur to a woman who finds herself intensely nervous and angry at her mate to blame him for not making her pregnant when she knows that she herself is the one who forestalled him in his efforts.

Putting the whole case in reverse you can understand better the reason for a man's natural dislike for the woman who asks him where he has been, what he has done, and where did he do it and with whom. He hates to be chained down although very often he has nothing to hide and wouldn't want to anyhow. It's simply that his nature is speaking, the nature of man which states that having impregnated one woman successfully, naturally he must repeat the action. His nature doesn't know if he did or didn't. It drives him on to greener pastures where he can do the same thing again. He's supposed to be like the bull who's been put out in the herd of cows. They each must deliver a calf for the end of the season. So although man sits politely behind a desk all day and brings home his paycheck and never wanders from the hearth, his natural nature is having a big argument with him over the fact that he's allowed himself to be chained down by one woman. No matter how happy she makes him and no matter how hell-bent he is on never becoming a father if possible, his nature knows he has cheated and that he should be out working for the future of the race by providing a whole lot of little bastards in all sorts of distant fields.

Nature knows nothing about the law or divorce or marriage or economics. If we face it, nature really is very igorant. She hasn't bothered to keep up with the times, knows practically nothing about what's going on. Nature still interests herself in the most basic facts of life, little things like toileting, eating, sleeping and getting pregnant. I don't think nature is very interested in love affairs or emotional rapport or even talk-outs. I think communication doesn't mean a thing to nature. A healthy attitude, together with an energetic interest in that game which leads to babies, is about all nature cares about and most of us pay the price for it in one way or another. Nature is nagging away inside all of us, full of disappointment that we haven't had a litter of six every ten months and that the fellow who has failed to get us in this state isn't out busy trying to do the same thing to somebody else all the time.

Both man and woman suffer from frustrations of their failure to be total rats to each other. She by providing him with more children than he can afford to support and he by being disgustingly unfaithful to her at every opportunity. It would be an impossible world if we did play straight with nature and it's an impossible world while we don't because she isn't going to let us get away with it without considerable suffering. Angry, nagging, frustrated women and disappointed, silent and depressed men —everyone fishing around in his medicine cabinet for a pill or some other answer to that very normal function called getting together and getting a result.

So though it's a sad state of affairs, neither man nor woman can be blamed for it. She must be mean to him in every possible way because she is being thwarted in her continual quest for maternity,

And he in turn is equally thwarted by having his freedom snatched away from him and in being possessed. The woman takes his paycheck, dictates his diet, orders his social life and in general saps his strength, and so he must loathe her. He doesn't want to feel this way but he can't help it. For him, the fun is in the hunt; once he's caught her and it's over, it's over. It's normal for him to scorn what he's already conquered and this is shown in his disinterest in the female right after the sexual act. She expects him to stay cuddly, to keep telling her how lovely she is and how much he cares for her, when all he really wants is a chance to roll over on his back and start snoring. And so the male has his own revenge by often treating her rudely, spending as much time as possible playing golf and poker with the boys or going on hunting and fishing trips, which of course are his natural pastimes. He talks to her as little as possible and if he's the rougher type or one who gets nasty when drunk, he may occasionally punch her around a bit.

I don't believe the male deliberately sets out to be cruel to his wife any more than she plans her wild bouts of pre-menstrual tension. The truth of the matter is—men and women are natural enemies, like jungle animals, instinctively clawing out at each other—and paying a few dollars for a marriage license can't change these basic facts of human nature.

7 { MARRIAGE IS
A SECRET SORROW

You have probably had the surprising experience when you are close friends with people; you know them quite well; you see them often; they always seem to be quite happy, well adjusted, getting along fine until all of a sudden, one day, you learn they're getting a divorce, and all their friends say, "But I always thought they were so happy! Whatever went wrong suddenly?" In my opinion, nothing ever goes wrong suddenly. It's been going wrong steadily for years and people have been putting a bright front on it.

I have two marriages behind me. I hardly remember how I got into my first marriage, but getting out of it was fairly easy because I had met James who was my second husband. He stuck around for about four-and-a-half years until eventually my first husband said to me, "Wouldn't it be a good idea if instead of him looking for a new apartment, I'd look for a new apartment and you and he move in together?" Which is exactly what we did and we later arrived at an agreement for a divorce. James and I got married almost immediately after that became final.

Throughout the over-twenty years of our marriage, most of our friends thought we were fairly happy and got along pretty well, though most of them probably wondered why James put up with it. I think the general concensus of opinion was that I probably was a big bully who ran the whole roost and usually had an admirer around whom James, for some reason or another, tolerated. When we broke up, everybody was surprised because they thought, "Why would they break up when obviously they were getting along so well with that peculiar set-up they had?" There's no way of accounting for why you suddenly reach a point where you can't go on together any longer.

I shouldn't hold up my own marriage because it wasn't a perfect example. I don't know whether we would have been married at all had there been no war and had we not been running a chicken farm and had we not been in a position of having to travel as man and wife for the armed forces. We did so because it was part of our military service and to do so you could not register under an assumed name and therefore really the right thing to do was to be married. I don't think either of us minded particularly being married. We were already living together and had been for some years and the idea of adding a marriage to it meant nothing one way or another. It only was a convenience. Yet, for many years I think we probably were quite happy within that rather odd convenience. However, gradually over a period of twelve or fifteen year, whatever had been in it faded away and we were only polite to each other.

I don't think we ever had a real argument in all the years we were married. We hardly ever disagreed about anything. We had a complete ability to understand each other's mental attitudes and laugh at each other's jokes, which is to my mind a most important thing in marriage anyway because it is the most lasting. If you can't laugh at each other's jokes, there's just no point in trying. However, that still doesn't preserve a unity of thought. And we both found we could flit through our lives fairly well without hurting each other too much or without encroaching on each other's preserves too much. But I think from the time our first child was born, the marriage took a terrific set-back and I think that's so in most cases.

One is not entitled to generalize because of his own experiences but I have noticed invariably after a couple of children, the average not-very masculine man shies away; he's not too keen. He looks forward to the first one with great glee, is thrilled to death when he sees it around for a while, and then when the second one is on the way, somehow or other, the whole thing disintegrates. In my own case, I would say the arrival of the first child dented the marriage considerably. First of all because it gave me a new interest which did not allow for driving James to and from work. I had been doing so before and therefore it was a great deal of attention that was removed from him and given to the small fry. From then on, the child had to be considered when travelling and so we couldn't travel easily; we couldn't make films abroad, or at least we couldn't go with him and I wouldn't go without the child; so he had to live a very separate life after that. Until then he had been wrapped more or less in a cocoon. It was inevitable that some time in the future another cocoon maker would come along and issue cocoon after cocoon for him, especially since he was as a film star in a rather exalted position.

As a man gets older, he often tends to fall madly in love more and more frequently and sometimes his madly-in-loves may last two years and sometimes only a few months, but they always are slightly overboard and this accounts for so many middle-aged divorces. I think in our case we hit a rock when James fell madly in love. He'd always fallen madly in love with his leading ladies but usually they were married or busy or had no real designs on him, or he had no real designs on them, and so it fizzled out. Eventually he came to a situation where, whether she had designs on him or not, he had designs on her—and she was young. He pointed out to me, "I don't think I could marry her because I don't think I could make her happy." I found this a rather insulting comment and I wanted to say, "What about me? Are you making me happy?" But that had not entered his head.

Until that time I had always had friends, let's say, whom he liked, but then I made the mistake of having a friend he didn't like. Strangely enough none of my friends were ever challenged except the one he didn't like, and once that happened we were off to the races in no uncertain terms. Divorce loomed up as inevitable, because I wasn't going to change; he wasn't going to change; things had gone from bad to worse, and we certainly no longer had anything to say to each other. This is what I think happens in most marriages. It gets to a point where there is nothing to say. Women usually try to make conversation at mealtime so it'll seem there's a family atmosphere, but it's an awful strain on the woman

75

and hardly worth it. She would be happier having a boiled egg in the privacy of her own room, not having to struggle through, "How was it today, dear?" and not listening to the answer.

I think it's possible, but unfortunately I can't prove it statistically that opportunity is the key to whether people leave their marriages or not. I personally doubt there is one happy marriage except for where there are so many children, so many responsibilities, so much work to be done and such solid unimaginative people that they never question the fact that they're stuck with each other until the day they die because it wouldn't occur to them to ask, "Is my marriage making me happy?" I think leisure leads people to wonder, "Am I happy every minute? If I'm not happy every minute, then my life is a failure and my marriage is a flop."

Naturally this is a very high expectation but most people expect a great deal too much from everything. A few hundred years ago, if one movie had been shown—the lousiest one we could find today —the people all would have said it was the most fascinating, fantastic, marvelous thing that had ever been created. Now we're satiated with opportunities for entertainment and for gratification of every conceivable kind. We don't even have to cook our own meals because we can buy one in the market, shove it in the oven and in a short time, have an adequately good-tasting dinner. There's no real hard work attached to anything really, and marriage, although it should be hard work, seems to come under the heading of Pleasure and Entertainment. It is expected to supply a continuous form of gratification, and when it fails, like when one or another of the parties are ill or out of work or depressed or negative in general attitude or barren or sterile or uninteresting in bed, or interested in somebody else who's not supposed to be in the bed, or who isn't contributing enough chit-chat around the house, or interested in hanging the pictures, or showing pleasure at the sight of one's new hairdo—the marriage collapses.

It's probably very much in our attitudes. We ask of marriage something that marriage never could supply in the first place, because if we can't supply it ourselves, obviously another person can't supply it. So the expectation is too high and the delivery rate too low. Most people who are in a position to have a choice, get out of the marriage. But most people do not have the choice; they have no place to go. They have to stay with it, and that is where I think the so-called happy marriages are found,—in the homes where there is no possible way out. The people who are sort of arguing with themselves as to whether or not they should take the chance to get out are the secret unhappy ones who are putting a bold face on it; the really happy ones are those who are too broke to even consider it.

8 { MARRIAGE IS A PUSH BUTTON AFFAIR

Recently they worked out the idea of building **IBM** machines in which they can pop the details of your background, your foreground, and your shape and your size and your this or that, and your wishes, your hobbies, and the fun there is in you, into one little slot. And then take similar data on someone of the opposite sex, and slip it into another slot, then swish it all around together like in a brandy glass, and out will come the right answer, such as,—this one is mismated and this one is right to be mated. In other words, you can find yourself the perfect soul mate by letting the computer work the whole thing out, finding enough things in common and enough of the same background to make it the right setup.

I think if we ever depend on that method, we might as well wash out mating altogether. There's practically no purpose to it if you rule out the emotional feelings that people have for each other which can't be computed and never make sense anyhow. The whole idea of mating for the sake of mating brings it down to the brass tacks of "Who's going to father my young?" and "Who's going to keep my bed warm?" and "Who's going to pay for my keep?" From a woman's point of view, at any rate, there are just those three things. (But if that isn't all there is to it, then it is something much more, something that can't go into a slot machine.)

With a man, it's a question of "Who's going to be there with my warm dinner?" and "Who's going to cuddle me when my toes are cold at night?" and "Who's going to pander to my pride, see that my shirts are clean and love me no matter how stupid and egotistical I show myself to be?" I suppose such items could be satisfied in a slot machine, but the other item, the one that makes it all worthwhile, never can be. So if you're looking for that intangible something, you might as well forget the computer and just keep to yourself, living a self-centered life gazing at your own face in the mirror, (which always is the nicest face you ever see anyway and the friendliest.) Either you give up the whole idea or go back to the old, old system of sniffing around in the outer world until you find someone whose sniff is better than anyone else's. That is all love is anyhow, and the only reason, it seems to me, for mating in the first place, as we've now done away with the biological necessity of reproducing ourselves. Naturally we do all the lead-in, but we don't have to have babies as a result. We have birth control; we have abortion. We've never had self control really, and we're not likely to bring that in now. Why waste one's life on a silly thing like self control?

It would seem to me that because we've living in a machine age, we are trying to bring machine tactics even into our emotional living. We are becoming robots and will become more and more so. The state might as well take over breeding and maybe set up housing estates where women who have been impregnated can go and lay their eggs and have them farmed out with experienced farmers who understand how to herd young from one grade to another. The mother might as well walk away and forget all about it. Especially if her mating was arranged by a slot machine.

In the past there have been all kinds of methods of trying to get people together. There was the old fashioned matchmaker and there's the more recent psychologist who tells you, "It's no good your marrying this man because he comes from a Nordic background and you come from a Southern background and therefore you'll never be able to get along together."

All the rules he states were made to be broken because that's the way life is. The most unlikely couple are the happiest and the most likely and perfectly matched pair can't get along at all. I've often thought, as a rule of thumb, people tend to marry or love one of two types—either someone who's exactly like himself or someone who's exactly the opposite in every possible way. They are fascinated, bewitched and really taken with one or the other of these alternatives, and everything in between that might be reasonable will never work. Love doesn't work at any pitch at all except the extreme. It is a wave length that we can't ever pin down. In matchmaking, the friendly matchmaker would look for a suitable widow or a suitable young woman or a suitable income bracket lady with a dowry to fit the needs of the man who was pursuing the possibility of marrying. He had a farm that needed repainting and therefore he required a woman with five thousand dollars. It was as simple as that. He'd find a woman with five thousand dollars and no matter how unattractive and unappealing she was to him, he'd have to take her anyhow because it wasn't the woman at issue, it was the money. And it was another businesslike situation when a woman reached the awful age of twenty-five and realized she was on the shelf forever, (this was far in the past, of course) and had to hunt for a lonely widower with seventeen children so she could step in and fill the breech. But those forms of marriage were really careers—the finding of someone to fill the void in one's business or social life. They had nothing to do with love. That isn't what most women want, or really the thing that will hold a man.

Let's see if we can work out what is behind the computer system—what's the thought behind it— and what was the thought behind the matchmaking system. That was an effort to put together two people who required each other for certain purposes, whatever those purposes were. On the assumption that when they had made the deal, eventually love would follow, and it is considered quite possible that in many cases love did follow. However, it's difficult to know. Love means different things to different people. For instance, we all know that when an ugly, old, scruffy dog comes into your house, you say, "I don't want him. We don't need him. We can't have another dog." He stays overnight and the next day you say, "Poor old thing, well, maybe we'll let him stay for a week or so and maybe we'll find a home for him," and then he stays, and although everybody snarls and growls any time they see him and you say, "Oh, we shouldn't have let him stay," still gradually he takes on a familiarity which substitutes for affection. If he should leave, you'd say, "Oh, has that old dog gone?" with a certain regret. Why, that was part of one's home! You didn't particularly like him while he was there but nevertheless you got used to him, and getting used to things is half the game. The habit of loving one's parents. The habit of saying, "Yes, sir" to one's father. The habit of deferring to the boss, all these are probably much stronger than any other feelings we have. We are creatures of habit and we form unbreakable habits even about the things we most dislike, and I think that may account for a lot of those marriages where "love" followed. It wasn't so much love as habit and need and dependency and acclimatizing oneself to a certain routine of life which we easily do because we are by nature a herd creature rather than a solo act.

In any case, love being different as it is to different people, the kind of feeling a person can have for another person is a totally individual one. There are people who cannot possibly love anybody. No matter what they do, they always are in love with themselves although they don't recognize it and they always feel they are put upon by the world around them and the people they mix with and live with because they blame others for their own lack. They don't realize that the missing link is something that they are unable to feel. And I'm talking about love for anything. Love for one's children, love for the world around one, pity or sympathy for the state of others. It's a totally individual thing and something that those who cannot feel compassion or love, cannot understand and sometimes don't realize exists. They feel they've had the bad luck to always be with such rotten people that such a feeling never awoke in them. It was always killed before it got anywhere.

It occurs to me that one of the hopeless things about mating today is that it will get worse because of the increasing aggression on the part of women. In my opinion, that's an expression of the inability to love. In Hollywood, it's particularly noticeable but I assume it's growing all over the world—the mod costumes, the immodest exposure of all one's most personal attributes at a very early stage of a relationship—obviously these are aggressive actions rather than passive or placid ones. Women are no longer the passive and placid creatures they once were or were supposed to be, but nevertheless, nature's indication to us has always been that the woman is the receiver and the man is the giver or the aggressor. By nature a man must select those whom he wishes to mate with and must make the effort to overcome or overpower or over entreat her

85

into giving in to him. Now if a woman takes that out of his hands and makes the first, second or third move, he has no place in her society really, and she in turn never receives the necessary flattery or compliment of his efforts toward her and, therefore, she never can respond to him as she would if he had selected her and made his own efforts to obtain her. My guess is that as a woman tends to get more aggressive, so she becomes less sexually minded and less able to be pleased by a man and less able to love him or to be gratified by anything that he offers her. It's never enough. If you go out and pillage it for yourself, you criticize what you get, whereas if something comes and pillages you, you realize that in spite of what a dreary thing it may be, it chose you.

I think a woman who is capable of sexual passion is incapable of sexual aggression because it's against the nature of the specie. A woman who is capable of making contacts with men she doesn't know is really not much of a woman. This type is perfectly able to call a man she doesn't know on the telephone and try to make a date with him either because he's famous or has a big car or a bad reputation, or she's seen him drunk in some nightclub picking up the check and she figures he is fair game. Now these are the actions of a prostitute, but the girls who do these things today don't have a particular price. Their price may be only a drink; it may not be even that much, so actually they are offering themselves free to men who have shown no possible interest in them. What's more, such a girl isn't particularly abashed when the man turns her down. She just shrugs and says, "He must be a fag."

I've always had a nightmare that one of these fine days—I hope it won't be in my time or in my daughter's time either—there will be a great big factory where they bottle the seeds that make babies and stock them in every drugstore. Where you could go down the line and choose a tall blonde Swede or a short red-headed Irishman, or an early-graying American, or whatever your particular fancy may be. Then you could take the bottle to your doctor's office and say, "This is the date when I shall be ovulating, so will you please inject me with this product I just bought at the counter because this is the kind of child I'd like to breed." In other words, motherhood will, I think, continue but fatherhood will be dispensed with entirely and men will be valuable only for the support, fun and games they can offer, but they won't be at all necessary in the great big business of reproducing ourselves.

Somebody said to me the other day that the proof that woman is the most important sex is in the simple fact that, if every man in the world died tomorrow and there was not one single man left, the world still would continue because there are enough pregnant women right now to rebuild the earth all over again. The new youngsters would grow up and start the whole game over. But if every woman died tomorrow, the world would come to an end because man cannot recreate his kind. However, the female of the specie is recreating so often, so thoroughly and so productively in so many places at once, nothing on earth can ever destroy her matriarchal importance in the world.

9 { MARRIAGE IS NOT A FREEWAY

Probably one of the most embittering situations within marriage is the relationship of the parties that exists for whatever financial gain they may have. For instance, if a man marries a woman for her money, she's basically bound to resent him unless he's the most wonderful creature the world has ever brought forth, and there are none exactly like that. And he will resent having to go to her for money. The best thing she can do is split it with him right away because he's going to get it anyhow, and, in the heat of love, usually a woman is willing to give whatever is required. However, as time goes by, it becomes an aggravating situation and love often disappears. Similarly with the opposite situation, when a woman marries a man for financial support, which is the reason most women marry, she resents having to go to him for each little something she needs. And if a man gives her an allowance, he's always a little afraid she's saving some of it behind his back for a rainy day, or if he doesn't give her an allowance, then she has to get him to okay everything she requires and she feels too dependent. While they're locked in each other's arms, those dependencies don't matter, but when the physical part of their love affair begins to fade a little, the financial aspect becomes extremely important. And the matter of pride involved in having to ask for something bothers them. The matter of pride involved in having to give something in return for love also becomes a bothersome detail.

I think possibly the only financial situation that really is satisfactory to both parties' point of view is when the husband makes sufficient to live on and support the family without killing himself, and the wife doesn't overspend. They stay within their budget. Then it is possible for both parties to be fairly content with each other. He with her for her budgeting ability and her lack of demand on him, and she with him for his support and because she's comfortable enough to make life worthwhile. But, it demands a fairly placid type of character in the nature of both parties. Man, by the very nature of the beast, usually wants more than he can get. And woman, by the nature of her greed or her natural acquisitiveness, usually wants more products than she actually needs to be happy.

Possibly the reason that poorer people's marriages last longer, is because there's not enough credit available to them to get into real trouble, and their major occupation in life is concentrating on just getting by, rather than asking for, fighting for, dreaming of too much, and going in over their heads. Middle class people, I think, probably have a very strong tendency to spend more money than they possibly can make inasmuch as they always have heavy mortgages, large insurance payments and plenty of "unpaid for" electrical appliances including cars, which may not be electrical yet but they come under the same heading.

When you get into the so-called upper crust, where money flows, the troubles are enormous. Every woman wants everything and every man wants to escape without paying for it, if possible. Not that anybody, either man or woman, resents paying for something while great happiness is coming his way. This is at the height of the love affair or the beginning of the romance or the beginning of the marriage if the marriage is a good one. It's later when other things have crept into it—general dissatisfaction, dislike of each other's habits, quarrels over in-laws, friends, children, animals, places to live, places to go for holidays, etc. There are an endless stream of things that people can have quarrels about. In fact, there's practically nothing they can't have quarrels about. And into this infiltrates the ugly thing about, "Well, I'm paying for it" or, "Well, I can't pay for it," which is even worse. And obviously, love flies hideously out the window and angry people have to share that double bed at night.

A notable example: Let's take Lady X who had been married several times, usually to men who could at least provide some kind of support if not massive support, and although she was capable of supporting herself to some extent, it was never to the point where she would be satisfied. (There are certain women who never do like to support themselves. They always feel that it is the duty of the world to give them whatever subsidy they need, especially if some man is going to take a little of their favors.) Lady X married for the fifth time a man who had all the apparent appearances of wealth but didn't happen to have the money. Naturally when she found out that he had only a small income, she was bitterly disappointed and resented tremendously the enormous amount of cash she had to lay out to support her big home—with him in it. A love that was wildly passionate in June, was as dead as a doornail by the end of July, not to mention that a hatred such as seldom is seen on earth had sprung up between them. It had nothing to do with his appearance or manners or his ways. If he had been rich, all would have been well. She would have loved him for at least as long as the wealth lasted.

It's known statistically that more divorces are caused by financial problems than anything else. Adultery is a very minor consideration compared with the great hatreds and furies that have caused people to seek the court's help. There's nothing a woman resents more than finding her husband is filtering off some of their income playing pool, horses, helping his old mother, or especially if he's helping some new girl friend. (It isn't so much that he's giving the girl friend what should come to the marriage bed, it's that he's giving her some of the cash that should have been spent on the home front.) It's also well known that the fightable items in a divorce case are far more often the valuables than anything else. Couples could separate on an equal basis if only there weren't those little things to fight over—the ashtrays, the furniture, the closets full of rubbish that nobody wants, and the income that one of the parties is going to have. Some men sue women for their income—their future income—and many women sue men for alimony and then put off marrying other men they really could love, simply because they don't want to give up the alimony they're collecting from the previous skunk.

Apropos of the fairness of alimony in general,

first of all, to clarify the whole thing, it should be obvious that the children must be supported at all costs, if the state isn't going to do it. I personally recommend that the state do it because that would save the legal fees and prevent the couples from carrying on in court they way they do now. But the children never should be the victims. If there's money in the family, no matter whose it is, the children should be allocated that part which is of necessity theirs. There's no reason why a man should be allowed to dump one collection of children and move on and lay another few eggs in another nest and probably dump those also and leave their support to the wife, her father or whomever she can catch who will take care of them. I think it behooves a man not to have a family at all if he doesn't think he can support them and doesn't intend to support them. However, there are all kinds of circumstances. Supposing when a couple marry, the wife is earning good money and the husband is earning poor money and they survive together for some years. When they divorce, if there are no children, in my opinion there should be no alimony to either party—unless the wife has given up her earning capacity. This is where I feel the law has had to favor women. Often when a woman marries, even if she was earning just a pittance, who knows what it might have grown to had she continued working? If the marriage has lasted twenty years, which could be considered her most productive period both from the point of view of having a family and of creating a career, I think she's entitled to considerably more—as long as she did not work during the marriage. However, if the wife continued to work during her marriage, even if she had children, I think all a man should be asked for is child support, unless they have accumulated a great fortune, and she had some part in the creation of it. If she was a working woman, presumably she concentrated somewhat on herself and her own career and was not necessarily a particularly important part in helping her husband's career. If, on the other hand, she retired and gave him her full attention, entertaining his dreary friends, his boss, his clients, and other people who might be useful to him, then she probably had something to do with helping him along.

Many wives do give up their careers such as they are, and concentrate on helping a man, but in actual fact they often hinder him by being so slow, boring and illiterate, they hold him back and impede his progress rather than help it. So it's a very moot point as to whether a woman is actually a necessity and is as much a help as she often thinks she is.

However, I believe the courts could easily grade

95

what a woman is entitled to by the number of years she's put in, by the amount of time she has given up her own work to please her husband, and by the amount of money he actually makes. A woman who is still in her early forties shouldn't be considered a dead issue just because she's been married fifteen or twenty years. If she has young children at home, obviously she needs some support. But she can't just retire and live on alimony. She shouldn't because that's a way of saying, "My life is over."

Many men are willing, if they have enough capital, to give a woman a huge slice just to get rid of her—anything, in fact, to see the end of her. But some will fight it out to the death through the courts to try and preserve even the car that's in the garage and to prevent her from getting anything at all.

Now, on the other side of the coin, there is the man who wants to sue his wife for support, which is more uncommon than the reverse but it's not too uncommon. However, here again, I don't think it makes much difference whether it's a man or a woman. I think it's a question of the circumstances. If a woman marries a man who supposedly is going to support her, and the girl's father in the meantime leaves her a fortune and they both go around the world and spend some of it and then decide to be divorced and he decides to sue her for part of it, I think this is completely uncalled for and unfair. I don't see why he should cash in on what her father worked for. But if she marries him and says, "Look, darling, I don't want you to be a stockbroker, or a doctor, (or whatever he is,) I want you and me to go and live in the West Indies because I'm so rich. Daddy made me successful, so why don't we spend our lives having fun?" Then I think she has coerced him into giving up what he was doing, just as he in the reverse situation might have caused her to give up what she was doing, and therefore, he's entitled to a reasonable chance to get a new start. And again I think that it depends on the age of the person. If he is in his forties or fifties, he still can get started again. If he's in his nineties or hundreds, he hasn't got too far to go anyhow.

As a particular example—in show business it often happens that a woman who is on the way to becoming a star or, at least, has somewhat of an earning capacity, may marry a man who is doing a little something and he decides to give up his job as an agent or whatever it is, and concentrate on managing her career and taking care of her. And then, five or six years later when her career is doing fairly well, they may split up and she wants to go her own way.

In this case if the man decides to sue her for alimony or some of her income, he's considered something of a rat and people are shocked, surprised and amazed that she ever put up with him in the first place. And yet, without him, she might never have gone as far as she did. It's very difficult for a woman to get along on her own in show business or in any other business. And therefore, if the man has given up all outside activities and concentrated on her, he has every reason to believe he has a partial investment in her career. Now she may be able to go on to better things without him, but who knows if she ever would have got this far except for him? I think that he deserves, if he has devoted his entire effort on her behalf, a portion of her accumulated capital. If a woman can expect half the capital in a community property state, the man probably is entitled to the same. Half of that which was acquired during the course of the marriage. I think, also, he is entitled to a few years of future support or a percentage of her future income until he can find his place again in another field. If there are children and one of the parents has done all the earning, then, obviously, that one should take the major responsibility for at least the first few years after the marriage breaks up. (In the event that the other party later gets into a position where he can offer some support, then the responsibility should be divided equally between them.)

An illustration of the turnabout situation in Hollywood concerns a young actress who was on television for many years. When she married, she and her husband made a deal that she would continue with her career since she had a more interesting one than he did and he would stay at home and take care of their ranch and eventually their children. So she went to work and earned their keep and he took care of the home responsibilities and their marriage seemed happy. When the time comes for them to divorce—as it usually comes to most married people—that man certainly should receive a share of the actress' income. There is the chance that this particular marriage may not fail, just because of their special arrangement. Sometimes that particular situation holds together a marriage that would fall apart otherwise. I'm thinking of a very successful screen and TV actress who once won an Academy Award, and her manager husband. Whenever I see these two together in public, I get the impression their marriage is not an idyllic one. Yet, they stay together and keep a smooth running home for their children. I believe the reason for this is that she is now dependent on him to manage her affairs—(business affairs, that is. I have never heard rumours of another kind involving either of them)—and he is dependent on her to have something to manage. Dependence on each other seems to me to be as good a basis for keeping a marriage going, as any other.

So you see, I don't think the old rule and regulation that the man has to be the breadwinner is necessarily right. It applies to some men but it doesn't apply to all men. Some men are absolutely created to be both the breadwinner and the boss. Other men are perfectly happy not to be either. It doesn't make any difference to them where the support comes from, as long as it comes from somewhere. Personally, I'm convinced a true marriage demands that one or the other of the parties gives up outside activities. I think the good wife, the ideal wife, obviously finds enough to do within her marriage, taking care of home and children and a man, to make it a full time occupation and a worthwhile one. She doesn't need to be a secreatary or any other kind of career girl on the side. There's not that much in it for her, except for the feeling of being independent financially. But a decent man should recognize a good wife's worth and be prepared to make her independent financially anyhow. At least he will give her a living wage such as he would pay any housekeeper or helper.

But as I said, the same thing works in reverse. If a woman has a career that she can't give up because it's too important and too precious—as, for instance, a woman writer, performer or executive in some field where it's really valuable to her and something she really wants to do—and she marries a man who is in something he isn't particularly crazy about and isn't going anywhere much with it anyhow, it seems to me to be perfectly legitimate he should stop working and follow her star, such as it is. At least, they can be together and travel together and concentrate on one objective. I think the marriage where there are two careers in the family is practically always doomed to failure because of the fact that two people living together whose interests are very diverse naturally don't have half the chance of success as those couples who are concentrating on one objective. Obviously the major objective in the life of most women would be to have him please her. The major objective in the life of most men would be to have her please him. But both parties, if they are cunning enough, can pretend the major objective is the one which the other wants. (But most men aren't that cunning.) I think that marriage where both parties concentrate on one career certainly has a better chance of contentment than one where each party is travelling away by himself. Separations are never good from a marriage point of view. Sooner or later a separation results in not wanting to come home, for whichever one who is escaping.

It would be foolish to start talking about the ideal marriage because I'm not too sure there is such a thing. But suppose there is. I would say that the ones that work out the best are probably those where the woman is totally dependent and the man is totally independent and where a large or largish, by modern standards, family has been infiltrated into the group. The woman whose energies are used up in childbearing obviously isn't so busy worrying about her independence and although she may be bored at times, (which is not too likely if she's an energetic and thorough woman,) she will realize she has been totally fulfilled. Diverse careers within a marriage invariably lead to trouble and there are enough possibilities of trouble in any case in relations between two people. The great problem is for people to understand whether they have enough in common to make worthwhile what they jointly will need to do to preserve their marriage.

However, I think the law has been overly unfriendly toward the woman in some fields because often she has to fight like mad to get even the smallest pittance to live on. But, in general, the assumption that the male must pay for everything while the female must take everything is rather absurd and I think there's nothing more unfair than a woman who marries a man for a few years, does not have a family by him, and then expects him to support her for the rest of her life. There's no justification for that. It simply means that she is a parasite by instinct and has found it easier to be a parasite than to earn her keep in the proper course of events as a prostitute. A wife who doesn't love her husband actually is the same as a prostitute except that she doesn't receive cash for each performance. She receives a steady income throughout the time that she stays with him and probably from then on. Not to mention a split of community property. None of this, in my opinion, is very fair. What you put into something is really what you deserve to get out of it. It's hard for the courts to find out what people have put into their marriages or how much effort each person has made. But the time is part of it and the sacrifice is also part of it, and that's why I think it's extremely unjust that a man should suffer immense shame if he asks for part of the property that he helped to build.

There's a case in point of a well-known star who literally was incapable of working due to nervous breakdowns, drinking, drugging, etc. Then she was taken over by a tough fellow who knew how to get her back on her feet. (What method he used, heaven knows, but it was effective.) Soon she was working again, considerably better than she had before and much more successfully. No doubt he filtered off a certain amount of her earnings but he also made it possible for there to be any earnings in the first place. When they split up, the fight was considerable because he wanted what he considered his share.

There's another far better known case, that of

103

Elizabeth Taylor and Eddie Fisher. He gave up his career to travel with her, took care of her through her violent illness in London and on other occasions, and when they separated, it is presumed there was a fairly large settlement made on him, as there was on Sybil Burton. Both he and Sybil Burton had put in many years of helping and protecting the talent of the other party and so both were entitled to proper payment for the time they put in. Eddie Fisher has proven he is perfectly capable of earning a handsome living on his own and therefore two or three years out of his life devoted to his care of Elizabeth was not to be sneezed at. His earning capacity was still there, and similarly Sybil Burton has proven that she also was capable of doing very well for herself, as witness the enormous success of her discothéque, Arthur, which is being franchised all over the country. Why should either of these people have had to devote their time and energy to suffering, either by the help and support they gave the other party, or by the business support they were able to give them? Why should they have suffered financially when the time came for the inevitable break? Inevitable, I say, because after all, as we all should know, marriage is the first step toward divorce.

10 { MARRIAGE IS
      A DEEP FREEZE

I know very little about women except what I've
heard but in my opinion, there's never been a really
frigid woman in the world. I think a woman is not
roused by biological urges within her, nor by sex
demands within her, because a woman is a security-
seeking creature. According to nature, she's going
to be impregnated one way or another and so instinctively she makes safety her main concern. She's
a mental creature who lives off her thinking apparatus rather than her emotional apparatus, at least
sexually. She has to think, *I'd better not let him take
advantage of me or I may get stuck with this*. All of
her life, therefore, she cases for which is the best way
to go in order to be safe.

Very few men know anything about giving a

woman a feeling of security, other than by present-ing her with a diamond or a fur coat. Nice as such gifts are, they're not going to make her un-frigid in bed. They'll keep her happy and delighted while she's out wearing them but once she gets to bed, her freezing mechanism will start working again. Her nerves will begin telling her perhaps he really doesn't love her and perhaps she really isn't ade-quate. (With men being what they are, her doubts probably have a basis.)

At any rate, a small study of the art of flattery would get a man anywhere because a woman, to warm up to him and feel he is the most desirable person in the world (at that moment) must be put at her ease. A man flying out of his clothes and showing a hairy chest, leaping into bed beside her, ready for action, isn't going to reassure the average insecure woman. It's going to make her feel she's pushed into a situation from which there is no way out once she's gone that far. Very often he's not about to waste any time because he's squandered an entire dinner and maybe even a dance or two. Be-sides, he has to get up early. He figures he's done everything necessary—fed her, told her what fun she is to be with; he's laughed at two of her jokes, missed the third, then said, "Well, why don't we nip upstairs? It's already twelve o'clock and I can be home by one-thirty, which means I'll still get six hours sleep."

That's the way it goes and the average woman just can't respond to that. Naturally there are some technically proficient ladies who have a fetish right in their own minds and so are able to come to action with anybody anytime. They just close their eyes and visualize King Farouk or whomever they really dig. These women continue to have romantic affairs with myths instead of reality. But the usual woman, if she so much as opens her eyes to see who she's with, may close them again quickly and curl up and die, proving herself frigid both to herself and her mate.

It's well known that certain Latin races have always understood the big deal is—flattery. Those men use it in all forms. They bow and scrape; they kiss hands and make compliments which probably mean nothing. However, a woman at the point of being taken to somebody's bed will believe anything she possibly can. She doesn't want to feel the fellow is doing it only to get back the steak and potatoes he bought. She likes to believe he really thinks she is the greatest. Just one line isn't going to do it. If the man wants her to feel free and easy with him, he must tell he *all* the things she needs to hear.

As any doctor will tell you, there's no use in having a nasty, cold attitude when interviewing a patient. The person won't open up and tell the whole truth. He may speak of a few little things but he'll forget to mention some ghastly disease he happens to have in his lower quarters. A good bedside-mannered doctor will get his full confidence. The same principle applies to a man with a woman.

Those girls who are considered, and consider themselves, frigid, are caused, not born. A girl brought up by an over-strict or over-refined or over-shy mother gets the impression there's something dirty or wicked about sex and therefore she can't allow herself to indulge in it. A good man can break down such a woman but the average fellow, once married, figures he now can claim his prize and sets about to use it for all it's worth, with no idea of how to soften up an unwilling captive.

The key to de-icing a woman is in the man's behavior. It won't do to be rude to her all day and then hope to coax her happily into bed of an evening. He must woo her all the way until she feels completely comfortable and admired by him. This is most important to ensure a woman's sexual response. The few women I know who insist they've had great lovers, tell me those lovers were extremely conscientious when it came to talking. They may or may not have been able to come on with the action as well but their talk got them into some very tough-to-find beds.

A woman will hug the thought to her that he said this and he said that. She'll never forget his kind remarks and he always will seem to her the only understanding man the world has ever produced. In the same way, she never will forget his rude remarks and boorish actions. One small criticism, one suggestion that maybe her nails are too short, or he liked her hair better the old color, or her voice is too loud or too soft—just about anything that could be construed as disapproval, may put her right back in the cold frame of mind she had when she shoved the children out to school in the morning.

There's a story about a well-known film executive who had played around for years and finally met a girl he wanted to marry. They went on a picnic to a sandy beach and she was stretched out in her bikini when he leaned over and said, "Oh darling, you have a corn." She got up, put on her robe and left the beach. The engagement was off and she never spoke to him again.

That didn't mean she was frigid. It simply meant, as a woman she had to have her security settled first. She needed the feeling of being utterly acceptable, perfectly adorable, completely irresistible, and the only woman in the world he could enjoy. The mention of a corn was strictly out of line.

Similarly the man who plops into bed beside you and promptly tells you what a wow he was with that chick last week, and other success stories, is not going to bring you around to feeling anything except fury and disgust. Men seem to be absolutely unaware that women are creatures of extreme vanity (just as men are creatures of great egotism) and that they will stay frozen until that vanity is satisfied.

A shrewd male performer I know told me that men approach love with their eyes; they are excited by what they see. But women are enticed with their ears. If a man can't think of saying something reasonably enchanting, he is not going to do much to the average woman. He may give her all the gold in the world only to find she is having an affair with the chauffeur. Why? Because the chauffeur says, "Madam, you are the most gorgeous thing I ever saw in my life!" While the foolish man who is paying his salary never remembers to say anything.

That's a fact of life and I think it exists in every nation to some extent, and in every walk of life. The laborer who comes in from work and grabs hold of his fifty-year-old woman and says, "God, honey, I thought about you all day," will have her rolling in the hay before he knows where he is. Whereas, the fellow who stalks in, picks up the evening paper, or turns on the TV for the entire evening, and then says, "How about bed?" is going to get a mighty cold shoulder when he jumps in.

If she's being paid to be there, as wives are, probably she'll have to perform as best she can but he won't be pleased and eventually he'll go to a psychiatrist to complain, "What's wrong with my wife?" What's wrong with his wife is *him*—as many analysts point out. How can one persuade men that women must be flattered enough to give in feeling warm and cozy about it, and not feeling disgusting?

It's not a matter of being puritannical. It's just that the act of love, fun though it may be, looks ridiculous if you happen to catch anybody else at it. Any woman with imagination realizes she'd look pretty silly if two of her oldest friends happened to walk in. It just has to seem romantic for a woman, no matter what men like to think. Those women savages James Bond always meets, ever ready to throw themselves on a haystack and say, "Take me!" exist mostly in books and movies.

There are some women who may act that way because they're hunting madly for something that will make it all seem sense to them. Very few women really enjoy such behavior. In fact, medically, it's assumed that only nymphomaniacs—completely incapable of being satisfied by any man—are able to go to bed with just anybody at a moment's notice. They can't differentiate between one person and another, since none produces any effect on them. The woman who is capable of love differentiates very sharply. She knows immediately whether a man is acceptable to her or not. For financial security, she may marry someone who isn't, but even *he* could win her if he worked hard enough on making her feel really loved.

The same tricks apply to men, although they are not so often known to be frigid. A woman doesn't have to lure a man on to that extent because once a man gets into action—if he's capable of action—there's no stopping him. But a woman can put a man off by a lack of understanding of his little sexual foibles. Most men do have strange fetishes of their own. The trick of the sophisticated woman is to discover them and respond to them without making him tell you what they are. The whole gag is ruined if he knows it's all put on.

Some men, for instance, like to come upon you unaware—so you must act as if it's an accident. Some men like to find you lying down asleep in the dark, and so you have to pretend you haven't awakened. There are all sorts of angles that may please him and your job is to find out what they are and cater to them. The woman who comes into a room, immediately throws off all her clothes and leaps at him, ready, is usually slightly discouraging to a man who wanted a chance to woo her.

Also, you always can laugh a man out of bed. Mirth seems to kill all of a man's sexual power. One giggle at his expense and that's it—he'll never be able to look at you any more. He'll have to have psychiatric help, male hormones and a seventeen-year-old girl before he is able to do anything again.

Also, marriage can be chilled fast for both partners when they are inclined and allowed to issue criticisms on practically every subject. There's nothing worse than post-mortems after little teeny-weeny quarrels. You can build them up into great big things simply by trying to find out exactly why-did-you-say this and why-did-he-think-that. Nobody who wants his marriage or romance to last should try to have it out thoroughly. Let it go. You'll only make it worse by adding another insult to the previous batch.

It's terribly hard to overcome the cruel things that are said in the heat of passionate rows. It's terribly hard to ever love again a person who has given you a few basic insults. You may have to stick it out but the hurt remains and the feeling of distrust remains. Usually at those crucial moments when you ought to be thinking of something else, all of a sudden it flashes back: *He said I had a wart on my knee! She said my mother is a big bore and makes the lousiest apple pie she's ever tasted!* These little things, once said, never can be erased and will come back to haunt you in your bed.

I think the whole business of trying to understand each other by having out your disagreements is a terribly unsafe process because you may find, when you've analyzed enough of it, there isn't anything

113

you like about each other. Living phonily—if you've been polite and never spoken the wounding truth—you may be fooled into believing there are several acceptable little things, and it's all working to some extent. There's a moral to this thinking: practically never tell the truth if it's painful to anybody you hope to go to bed with in the future. A big lie will go much further for you and probably give you much more fun.

Both marriage partners should bear in mind that security in and out of bed depends on the feeling— untrue though it may be—that we are utterly loved at all times. We demand it of our parents and we demand it of our mates. If our mates don't come through with it, they may find us frigid or impotent, depending on which sex we are.

I think psychiatrists should stop analyzing people to find out where it all started. Instead, they should get down to exposing the fact that the human race is the most vain little peacock ever created—that every woman wants to feel like Lana Turner on a pedestal —and every male wants to believe he is Adonis. (They just can't understand why they don't look the part.)

Undoubtedly, if we all were given this little bit of insight during our prep school years, we'd be able to handle our romances and our marriages much more successfully.

11 { MARRIAGE IS AN OLD-FASHIONED CUSTOM

Apparently marriage has become obsolete. It was intended originally for a good purpose, to protect women from the maraudings of the male and his very easy flight in the night, (which is the natural instinct of the male,) and to try and keep him where he belonged while the egg was laid. It's sort of a long hatching process that the human specie goes in for, so it was necessary to come up with some form of enforced loyalty. The male had to be convinced it was terribly important that he sit around and watch his young be born and then wait for about fifteen years to see them grow up. Obviously nature never had such a foolish notion—nor does the male animal. He really has very little interest in watching his young grow up, unless he's having a marvelous time with the female who provided him with the young. Often by the time the young have grown up, he has another female who also is giving him a marvelous time and more young to grow up. Sometimes he's very clever or lucky and gets a female who doesn't have any young at all. Then he's much happier altogether.

So the system of marriage was invented for the benefit of the woman who had been so foolish as to listen to the endearments and the enticements of a male who said, "I shall love you forever and take care of you forever." And had allowed herself to become positively gigantic, gain fifty pounds more than her normal weight and give birth to a large, ugly, squalling infant who messed at both ends, very often at the same time. Somehow she had to find somebody to support this monster because she doted on it, that being nature's way of making her feel she's been paid off for all her miseries. The male of course has no part of that. His job is over about half a second after it all began. From then on he had to be inveigled into watching the result of what he'd done grow into its full horror. How was that accomplished? As far as I can see, various religions made the male feel terribly guilty if he didn't come through and love his wife and his young. Also a system was invented, making the woman the man's chattel and therefore just the same as his collar and studs and so on. He didn't want anyone else to have them, and so he must take care of them. He probably wasn't too crazy about the woman but as long as nobody else had her, it was okay. He would do his best to keep his claw on her while he looked around for something else to put his other claw on.

Well, obviously this hasn't worked through the ages because every so often man has managed to have two or three prongs out in various directions —two or three families growing up. The original wife—the first one who fell for the whole story— might have five or six young. In the old days, with good luck and bad hygiene, she died at an early age and he could replace her with something younger and fresher. However, because of medical advances as time went on, he got stuck with her; she lived to a ripe old age, in fact, is now outliving him ten to one. So he's in the embarrassing position of having to live his entire life before he's forty-five or he may not have it, meanwhile knowing she's going to live on, inheriting his wealth, until she's ninety or a hundred. That also is nature's idea—that women last out and men don't. There really isn't much use for the male after the first flush of youth but there's a great deal of use for females. First of all, they're hard-working, industrious—and men never are that. Men are ball game enthusiasts at best and drunkards at worst. The female has to join in some

117

of man's pursuits but mainly she will try to do a decent job of anything that's demanded of her because such is her foolish nature. She's a beast of burden who takes her burdens bravely and carries through with them.

In the early marriage situation, supposedly she was protected by being sold at a barter or in a bazaar. Her father would put her up for auction and if she was lucky, some ancient creep would buy her and take her home and support her and give her some decrepit young. She was terribly fortunate if some young stalwart farmer bought her and several other girls at the same time. Then, at least, she could share her problems with the other girls. If by chance her father was wealthy, he could give a sack of flour, two barrels of gold and maybe a good ancient picture by someone like Cézanne to the neighbouring farmer and ask him at the same time to take on his daughter. In this way she could achieve a home and the fellow would let her breed the sons he needed for maintenance work around the estate. So she earned her keep. Naturally she had no rights nor did she have any loyalty from him. She was just a possession.

In more modern times the situation was changed somewhat. The Catholic Church, I think, did a great deal for women in creating the Virgin Mary. They made a woman something to worship. They created "momism" really and in creating it, they created a deep love—in Catholic men, at any rate —for the mom figure. Of course it ruined their sex lives. Since all women were representative of "moms" the men weren't too sure if they were allowed to use them for any other purpose. In fact it's still a moot point whether Catholic men do use women for other purposes than as "moms" to worship. I think there have been a few who made the struggle, but the main body of Catholic men have a worried feeling that maybe they're not entitled to accept sex at all—at least if it involves a woman. They are inclined to believe that the bottle and the priesthood are much more fun because those are legitimate whereas desecrating a "mom" probably isn't cricket. However, provided there's a child a year, the men feel at least they have accomplished what nature probably intended. To them, the *good* marriages are those where there's a child a year for seventeen years and their mom dies of early old age brought on by too many childbirths, too much effort, and too little love. I suppose most people imagine if a woman has a child every year, she's had a great deal of love but in actual fact, she's probably had none at all. Just as soon as she's out of the hospital three months, he feels guilty again. I think generally the male's degree of loyalty in marriage today is based on the old time idea of ownership. *She's wearing my jewels and furs and therefore she really is my adornment. She proves that I am famous and successful because she's got a mink something or other, a huge bouffant piece of hairdo and several jewels that may not fit her but certainly denote wealth.* This makes her something to hang onto —his own modern day chattel. When he finds a better chattel he can discard this one because the law stepped in on behalf of Henry VIII and made it possible for man to change horses in as many mid-streams as he fancies. After the first few children he's perfectly entitled to decide that he really doesn't find a woman who has enlarged under his very eyes all that attractive. Also he's noticed she looks at him with a slightly different expression—less enchanted—and she doesn't seem to have quite the same faith in him, or the same belief in the stories he tells her. (Probably with good reason.)

All in all, the fact that the divorce courts are getting fuller and fuller and busier and busier is not too bewildering to anyone who has looked around and seen what a state marriage is in and who realizes what it was meant for in the first place, and how little it serves its purpose in the second place. The courts are full of all kinds of people—including youngsters who have been married for a year and a half and positively loathe each other with an undying hatred, and older people who have been married twenty, thirty, even forty years, and want desperately to escape from each other. It is understandable with the young couples who want to break apart and start all over again with someone new. It's harder to accept divorces of people who are in their sixties and seventies. But perhaps when people have reached the end of their endurance and realize they have very few years ahead of them, they think, *What's the point of putting up with the big struggle and pretending any longer? I'll get rid of him (or her) and at least have a few years of privacy.*

Actually, marriage today is a very inconvenient and unnatural relationship. If we examine, for instance, animal life, we find that the domestic animal suits himself as much as he possibly can—dog, cat and even guinea-pig. Each, when he feels like it, lies in the sun or gets in the shade, disregarding his family ties completely. This doesn't mean he does not have a friend to play with when he wakes up and feels like it—but his friends certainly won't get up and play with him simply because they're asked. They suit themselves entirely. In wild animal life, the animal is a very responsible creature. He must provide the meals for himself and for his young. He has to hunt and maraud and live as best he can, taking full responsibility for his own survival. Yet, he only does that which suits him. He doesn't force himself or expect anyone else to be cheery and chirpy when they don't feel in the mood. He doesn't force himself or anyone else to meet a time schedule. And he doesn't take it out on somebody because he overheard a telephone conversation he didn't like.

Man, who is supposed to have the advantage of a thinking mind, has only proven that a thinking mind is not an asset, especially in marriage. He has forced himself to conform to any number of little religious rituals that he figures are his duty. His life is built on what he ought to do rather than on what he wants to do. Though he has no guarantee he's ever going to have any other kind of life, he's absurd enough to throw away the one he has on habits that have been acquired in youth because of the conformity of the world around him. Very few people go through their lives doing what they want to do any time whatsoever. A grown up person, by rights, should be respected as an individual, just as you'd respect your dog or cat. When you find your cat curled up on a cushion, you avoid disturbing him if you possibly can. Not so your wife or husband. You bark at them, insist they have meals when they don't want to, and drag them to places where they'd rather not go.

Husbands, are supposed to come home directly from work—even though after a certain age, their sons are not expected to come home directly after school or work. Nobody would think of dictating to a grown up son whether he should stop off and play a game of pool, or chat with some friends on the corner; he's entitled to his freedom. But the moment this same boy gets married, his wife becomes much more of a dictator than his mother ever was. She has the right to demand and expect, and be heard from if he doesn't show up on the dot. He may not look at, flirt with, talk to any other woman without affronting her dignity and her peace of mind and any number of other foolish things that she's built up in a generation of ignorance of humane human treatment. And he, in turn, has the same dogmatic attitude. If he comes home and finds she isn't there, a big row develops. He is suspicious, angry and affronted because he's paying for this article and not getting full service.

There are some deviations to these rules. There are people who have worked it all out a little better than others—but the main body of married people make nothing but demands on each other, have no consideration for each other's right to be, and right to live, and right to think. In fact, they expect docile slavery from the person who is supposed to be a life mate. They also expect everything to be shared by the other person. Personally, I think it's impossible for any two people to share *everything* once the first flush of mad romantic sex has disappeared, and it always does disappear when there are problems—home problems, children problems, and health problems. The glow of glorious commercial health, such as is seen on every television screen: clean teeth, clean breath, newly done hair, no underarm perspiration, no early morning huff—like the way everybody would like to find it today, is not part of marriage. That's the situation you have only when a fellow rushes to his home after work and showers before he comes to see you and then takes you out on a jolly evening where he spends the entire time holding your hand under the table and gazing into your eyes. That's love. The moment it disintegrates into a big quarrel over who's side of the bed you're going to sleep on and if it were he who messed up the bathroom and used the last piece of toilet tissue or if it was your fault all the towels had been trampled on with sandy feet, that romance is going to take a bit of a dive. It takes a dive for everybody and I can't see how we can expect it to do otherwise when it is forced into such an outmoded institution as—marriage.

12 { MARRIAGE IS
FOR MAKE BELIEVE

The wretched situation that seems to develop in Hollywood so regularly is that almost everybody has one, two, three or four divorces. This is standard procedure. Nobody thinks too much about it out here. In fact, I remember consulting a press agent during the time of my own divorce and she said, "Oh well, it's something that happens every day. It's nothing to get excited about." I was somewhat excited about it because it was my divorce and to me it wasn't exactly something that happened every day.

Actually, I don't think people in the entertainment industry are more concerned with getting divorces than anyone else, except that the opportunity to get together with the opposite sex is a little easier here and the temptation is probably a little more obvious and the ability to pay for a divorce—which is a considerably expensive item for most people— is more commonplace here. Also, often one party becomes extremely successful and the other party doesn't, and there is that desperate thing about who's paying for what, and so they want to get out from under.

There are many marriages and broken marriages in Hollywood are inexplicable to everybody except the people concerned. Cary Grant once married a lady called Virginia Cheryl way back in the "City Lights" days, (Charlie Chaplin's film in which she was his leading lady,) and somehow that broke up. Then he married Barbara Hutton and that lasted only a short time. (A lot of people have married Barbara Hutton, although she isn't in the movie business. But there are other reasons, aside from her prettiness, for marrying her.) Cary went on to marry an actress named Betsy Drake, and then he finally married the love of his life—the great discovery on how to be really happily married—Dyan Cannon, and after the delivery of his first child, somehow or other that marriage broke up too.

But there were many of those late marriages by older men that didn't break up. Clark Gable's marriage to Kay Spreckles broke up only when he died. Tyrone Power's marriage to Debbie Loew broke up when he died. As did Dick Powell's to June Allyson. As a matter of fact, dying is as good a way to break up a marriage as any other.

Although Bing Crosby always had an extremely good reputation, he was a well-known Don Juan in Hollywood, and Dixie Lee Crosby lived in comparative obscurity for many years. In his defense it must be noted that she was a very sick woman and eventually died of cancer and then he went on to marry a young girl. But, there were many young girls who were bitterly disappointed that he didn't marry them because they each expected to be the next Mrs. Crosby. Another famous performer's marriage has lasted a very long time but he spends most of it away from home. One of the ladies that he enchanted married a couple of other men in quick succession in a desperate effort to find love and happiness, but after a while she gave up hope. Another long-lived marriage is Jack Benny's but he seems to be away from home a great deal too, playing violin concerts in all parts of the world. Groucho Marx and Eden seem to be a happy couple. She spends most of her time painting and studying acting. Desi and Lucy—they don't need to be identified with second names—both have gone on to happier situations than their marriage of many years. She married again; he married again; and there were so many millions between them that apparently they were able to part company in record good-natured style. If there's enough money to spread between you when the marriage breaks up, you can remain friends. The trouble starts when the money is short. That's when it's difficult for one to like anybody. As a matter of fact, most of Doris Duke's husbands and Barbara Hutton's husbands still like their ex-wives. Pity to think that the dollar is the only way you really can win love, but there's nothing like a rich woman and incidentally there's nothing like a rich man either, especially if he's generous. (Usually they aren't.)

Let's look at a few random Hollywood marriages. Anne Baxter went to the other side of the world, Australia, to settle because she found the only man she could love and it lasted about three or four years. And then, although she had nothing but good to say about him, she apparently couldn't take him as a husband. Connie Stevens and Jim Stacey were a typically well-matched happy young couple whose marriage lasted a week and a half or some such time. He was jealous because she was flattered by people on various films she worked in. She may make a great wife for Eddie Fisher. They've both had disappointments. The Joel McCreas separated, threatened divorce and for some reason or other, decided to have one more try at it after thirty years. I guess they figured that cutting their community property in two was just too much trouble. If the community property law was changed, probably almost everybody in the movie industry would get a divorce. Many a couple stays together because the husband is too stingy to split the property and he can always hope his wife will fall down the stairs eventually and break her neck and he will inherit the lot. And believe me, they really do hang on to the wild hope that something will wipe her out overnight and he will be in charge of everything. It's a shame to sacrifice your life rather than share your community property, when you probably could be very happy with some little eggroll somewhere or other.

On the other hand, there is Mickey Rooney, one of the most married men in Hollywood, who's had about five or six wives, starting out I believe with Ava Gardner, which is a nice way for any man to start out. (She went on to bigger and better things, Artie Shaw, followed by Frank Sinatra, every girl's dream of delight.) In the case of Mickey Rooney, it always seems to be the man who pays but he still keeps on trying to strike the perfect match.

The Gabor family is rather unique. Zsa Zsa, Eva and Magda have had ten husbands among them, and one child. Something was short somewhere obviously. The girls certainly didn't follow in their mama's footsteps since mama only had two husbands and three children.

Marlene Dietrich has one of the strangest marriages of our day and age. She's kept the same husband for about thirty-five to forty years, made no attempt to get a divorce, nor has he, but though they're very good friends, they never have lived together in the last thirty years. Not to my knowledge anyhow! Evidently Marlene decided that rather than start dashing in and out of the divorce courts, she'd just as soon have the safeguard of a good, friendly husband working out his existence in another vineyard. Probably she made up her mind long ago that she didn't intend to marry again, and, no doubt, he either decided to go along with her or figured he couldn't lose too much by being the consort, even in absenteeism, of so great a lady. However, what stands out about Marlene's situation is that she is the past version of what Julie Christie is today. Julie Christie has the gumption to come out and openly state that she travels with her "mate" or "mates." She lives with her mate or mates and presumably, every so often she may even change a mate or two. But the word, marriage, never comes into it and is not a part of her ambition for the future. She is capable of saying on a newspaper page that she is living in open sin with this man, that man, or the other man. In Marlene's day, she couldn't have said that and got away with it, and yet the situation was practically the same, so nothing much has changed. Marlene remained married to Rudolph Sieber but never went anywhere with him and she was constantly escorted by various romances that passed through her life. Nowadays a lot of youngsters have followed Julie Christie's lead, and many oldsters too. Like, for instance, Jeanne Morreau who openly stated in *Life* magazine that she enjoyed romance and love more than anything else, that she didn't particularly plan to marry again, although she would if the right lover came along, but while waiting for him she wasn't waiting alone. As a matter of fact, when you see the open way certain stars are conducting their love affairs, you have to wonder why it seemed so imperative to Elizabeth Taylor and Richard Burton to consummate their three year romantic entanglement with a Mexican divorce and Canadian marriage. After all, the world knew they had lived together and their acting price had up accordingly and it's difficult to see who the marriage ceremony was for.

But it isn't only Hollywood that has these particularly peculiar relationships. The Julie Christie situation is a typically European one and it's growing immensely popular over there. Probably people are getting sick of paying lawyers to help them out of their romantic messes. Sleeping with somebody is one thing; then when the bloom is off the rose or the gilt off the gingerbread, all you have to do is point to the door. It's a different thing if that little gold band is on your finger. Everybody sues everybody and the lawyers get rich.

Yet, even Hollywood has many long term marriages. I can't say whether or not they're happy because nobody knows what goes on behind the closed bedroom door and so nobody knows which marriages are happy until they hit the divorce courts. For instance, the Van Heflins. Twenty-five years of marriage and not a rumor or a scandal at any time. Then the sudden revelation. When they went out they certainly seemed happy. The Burt Lancasters have had a long standing marriage with a large litter of children. Norma Lancaster once said to me, "You know, of course, if you had tried, you could have stayed with your first husband. One can stay married to anyone if one makes up one's mind to it." I don't know if this was a hint as to her own frame of mind, but I know that it was true. If I had made up my mind to it, I could have stayed with my first husband. But there didn't seem to be much purpose to it.

The Dean Martins are another example of a large straggling family and an on-and-off marriage with plenty of rumors surrounding it. However, they've weathered many storms and presumably are still doing so. Many years ago I remember a party when Dean was being extremely entertaining and amusing and slightly over the eight, making funny remarks and enjoying the full attention of the room. I caught Jean Martin's eye and she said, "I wish he'd say something funny at home sometimes." No man is a hero to his valet and it's even less likely he's a hero to his wife. But it's strange how many performers are sullen and disagreeable at home, and come on like gangbusters when they get out on the town—the life and soul of the party, the jolliest man to have around. In fact, most people when looking at other people's husbands showing off at parties think, *Oh why couldn't I have had a man like that?* Well, the only thing I'm quite sure of is that if you had, you'd find he wasn't like that at home.

Among the apparently happily married are Rex Harrison and Rachel Roberts who seem to be a good example of soul mates. Rex has been through many hard times in several marriages and Rachel is on her second. Although to many people they seem a strangely assorted pair, to those who know them well, they seem perfectly adjusted and extremely happy. The marriage between Fred MacMurray and June Haver seems to be a good one, at least viewing it from the outside. He was a widower and she had gone into a convent to become a nun and then changed her mind. Obviously, they had some extreme mutual need at the time they met and married and it worked out.

The Danny Thomases too appear to share a

happy marriage. I've never heard any rumors about them. (That doesn't mean there aren't some but they just haven't come my way.) At least, they've stayed together long enough for their daughter Marlo, and other children, to grow up. And they're usually seen out together of an evening, as compared to some couples who invariably are seen out apart. The separate couples always have great alibis. Usually, she says he's had to work late and must get up early, or he says she's not well, has hurt her back. There are more women who don't go to parties because they've hurt their backs! Actually, he probably gave her a swat before they left the house and she went into a deep sulk and decided to stay home, giving him just the freedom he was looking for.

Despite some rumors I have heard about them, the Robert Cummings seem to have hit on some kind of mutual understanding. He has occupied most of his life swallowing vitamins and eating health foods, organically grown, and going in for youthifying exercise. It seems to have paid off. He looks young, seems healthy and they have stayed together—so far. Perhaps a mutual interest in *his* health and longevity can be a full life for a married woman.

There seems to be no complete pattern for the average marriage in Hollywood. There are those who've lasted out thirty years—who knows whether they're happy or not? And there are those who decided to leave Hollywood and thereby preserve their marriages. Some people here tend to marry often after very short romances followed by short marriages and quick divorces. And there are others who have longer marriages, averaging six or seven years per attempt, which means they do try to work at it, and probably went into it with high hopes that it would last forever. It's easy to be happy for the first five years. That's about the time most romances last and the person who keeps on having a five year marriage can wind up with a collection of some very happy marriages. All the fun of meeting and falling in love, all the pleasures of trying to work the whole thing out and all the delights of being constantly admired and brand new. When it stales a little, off they go for a divorce, and then a new one comes on the scene.

Ingrid Bergman has had about three or four marriages all lasting a reasonable amount of time. Bette Davis has had four or five, all lasting a reasonable amount of time. Rita Hayworth has had several, none less than five years. Joan Crawford and Lana Turner have had four or five. Evidently these people are no fly-by-night marriers. They marry repeatedly but they give each one a good chance to prove its worth. I notice that in television and radio, the tendency to marry very often hasn't yet infiltrated. This may be partly because television is a very rough racket where people work so consistently fifty-two weeks a year, they can't find time to change partners.

Then there are people like Greta Garbo who have never married at all, but it's not to be assumed that she has always lived a solitary life despite the cliché that she likes to be alone. It's to be presumed that the most sought after woman in the world (until Jacqueline Kennedy) was not entirely unromanced. Yet she didn't bother with the little gold band, or that license which costs two dollars (and that certainly isn't going to pay for any of our world wars.) I think a lot of marriages would have lasted much longer had they not been married in the first place. There's something about staying with somebody because you want to and because you think you should, rather than because the law tells you to. Everybody has a big streak of rebellion in him, and there's nothing more senseless than having a man be rude to you in a home that is mutually occupied but in which you feel you have no right to throw him out. And if you have the right to throw him out, you'd probably never think of it.

There are certain marriages that last a long time for entirely strange reasons. It has been said that if a man or a woman has any weird perversions and manage to find the opposite factor to fall in love with, once that perversion is in full operation in the marriage arrangement, either party, for obvious reasons, will be loathe to break it up. It's more difficult to find a mate who goes in for the odd game than it is to find somebody who just plays a straight boy-girl sex relationship. There are several marriages in Hollywood, and I'm sure there are several elsewhere, that are based entirely on the fact that the perfect mate for the perversion has been found. Many a woman has been able to rule the rooster satisfactorily because she knew how to take care of her husband's strange ways, or was at least willing to.

To try and put in a nutshell why Hollywood marriages break up maybe a little more frequently than those in the rest of the world, I would guess that besides being subject to more provocation from outside interests, and having the money to pay for divorces, they're affected by the nearness of both Nevada and Mexico as easy divorce sites. And the eagerness of that one lawyer per every square inch of territory that we live in.

13 { MARRIAGE IS
A SCAVENGER HUNT

There are many different motives for marrying. There are women who are starving and who'd marry anybody for a roof over their heads and a free meal, and there are women who have children to support and would marry anybody to get them supported. And there are men who are so unattractive and so ugly that their only way to get any female companionship is to marry somebody and provide support. But we're going to consider these the far-out cases. We may eventually find that perhaps these are the main body of people who *do* get married. Yet it would be nice to assume the average person has something more to offer and something more to seek.

It seems to me that the female invariably seeks—

especially if she's young—several things in the male. Someone to look up to and admire. (A man usually can destroy this quite easily after their marriage.) Someone to lean upon. (A man, as a rule, really has not been trained to be leaned upon. He's been leaning on his own parents for quite a while.) She needs someone who will make her feel beautiful and pure and lovely and worshipable and someone who will consider her a main adjunct to his life situation. (Well, not many men are able to give those things.) In seeking all these accoutrements for her own ego, a woman also wants to have her own home and wants to live well. She wants something akin to where her parents left off, rather than where they started. She seeks from a young man the same things her father had been able to provide for her mother in her old age. This is an unrealistic view, but most girls don't want to take a step down when they marry. They like to take a step up if possible, so they hope the fellow will provide them with all the luxurious necessities of life. On top of that, the girl expects the man is going to be—miraculously, overnight—a marvelously comforting and pleasurable lover. However, if he's a man who hasn't played around a great deal before marriage, he's not likely to have had much practice in being a marvelous lover, and if he *has* played around a great deal, he won't consider her much of a catch.

140

At any rate, examining her aims, very few of them are unselfish. She wants a home; she wants support; she wants guidance and help; she wants to be loved and admired; she wants to be given a name and taken around. She wants, in fact, everything the world has to give, and instead of earning it herself, she just wants it from a man.

Actually, this isn't such an unfair point of view, considering this is what she has been brought up to expect. Marriage has been for generations the aim for most girls. She's been taught to believe all she had to do was be a reasonably clean girl and a reasonably adequate cook, and all else would come as soon as a man arrived on her horizon, willing to take her over. From that moment on he would be responsible for her support for the rest of her life. Though times have changed somewhat and many women are earning a living nowadays, supporting themselves on a large scale, basically they still have the expectation that the man in their lives will provide them with everything. That's why some girls marry *only* for money. Those are the practical marriages in which certain services are returned for a commercial gain, just as in any business. It isn't a very wise basis for marriage. If you marry a man for financial reasons—if you don't love him and he really doesn't love you—imagine what your life is like. It isn't a matter of going out in fur coats and

141

driving around in plushy cars. It's what happens or doesn't happen when you go home together, during the hours and hours you must spend alone with each other. If you have nothing in common and no joy together, it's miserable. I don't think anybody can realize just how terrible the situation can be except people who have lived through such marriages. So you must never confuse the man with the money. If his money attracts you, really look the situation in the eye and say, *Now what do I really want? Is there an easier way to get it than enduring forty years of an unhappy marriage?*

There are men too who marry for money but not quite so many. Mostly because rich women, if they're smart, try to marry men who are equally rich, to be sure they won't be sued or robbed of their jewels and fortune, or have their egos crushed. Young writers, however, and actors—artists of every sort—sometimes look for a wealthy woman who will dish out her wealth in exchange for their charms while they are pursuing their artistic careers. In both sexes, there are those who will sell for only a very high price and those who will sell for a lower price. In either case, the people involved are likely to be quite unhappy.

Even aside from the financial angle, many women marry in desperation because generally a girl regards marriage as a necessity, that she must at some time or another, marry. If you ask any woman under thirty, "Are you going with someone, or engaged?" she will answer, "Well, not at the moment but I expect some day I shall get married and have a family." In our society, a girl can only have a family respectably if a man puts his name in front of hers with a "Mrs." If he doesn't do that, she is in disgrace and her parents are furious with her. On the other hand, if you meet a man who's been shrewd enough to stay unmarried and ask him if he's attached, he'll say, "Absolutely not!" Or he may lie in his teeth and say, "I'll marry when I meet the right girl." If he hasn't met the right girl by the time he's thirty, really there is no right girl for that man. Usually he is completely wrapped up in himself.

From the man's point of view, what does he need a wife for? If he has a marvelous family name and wants to hand down his crown, obviously he would like to rear a son or two. He really doesn't need a large brood of children. Men prove over and over again they aren't particularly involved with their children unless they happen to be enjoying mother of same. He certainly doesn't need a wife to keep the house clean because he can hire somebody for a dollar and fifty cents an hour to do that. If he wants to eat well, he's probably better off in the average restaurant than with the average home cooking. Besides, if he happens to be nimble and has been in the army or navy, he's probably learned to stick a TV dinner into the oven himself, so he isn't completely helpless in that department. Now when it comes to seeking female companionship (and I'm speaking of female companionship in its most intimate form) there's never been a shortage of that since the world began. The red light districts are out of fashion now because there's so much free opportunity for the male, there's little point in expecting him to pay anything. The only men who pay for such things are the ones who can't be bothered to spend more than twenty minutes on the whole job. The average girl expects to be courted at least through two martinis and a few kind words. A call girl who is being paid twenty to a hundred dollars, depending on the going rate, doesn't expect even a kind word and very seldom gets it. Then if a man does not really *need* to get married, what can he be seeking? There must be a little something that makes a man feel it's worthwhile to take on this hideous responsibility of supporting somebody for the rest of her life even though he's already seen what her mother looks like at fifty, and fears that his girl at her age may look the same. He must be seeking some kind of emotional response, a place where he will feel he belongs, where he'll feel tied in with people who live in the same district, where he'll have opportunities to entertain his friends at home. He wants to feel there's someone who cares for him when he has a nasty cold in the nose. And we all know what cowards men are when they have a cold in the nose.

But a man shouldn't look upon marriage as a convenience any more than a woman should. He shouldn't consider the woman he marries as a laundress or a maid to get his breakfast at six-thirty in the morning or for any other purpose he deems fit at the time. That's a wrong approach to marriage. Marriage is something entirely else—or should be. It should be a mating of the souls—a deep and lasting *friendship* between two people who really *like* each other. I know love is wonderful but I don't think it should have anything to do with marriage. I think love usually flies out the window as soon as marriage comes in the door. Marriage is the biggest killer of love, in my opinion. The very familiarity of it—the necessity of being there —the hold—the chains—the gang warfare of it— take away all the spontaneity, all the wonderful things that come with love. You can love someone and you don't need to put a chain on him; you don't need to put a chain on yourself; you don't need to argue it or prove it—it's there. But the moment there is a certificate to prove it, a ring to bind you, the right to ask questions, the right to be complaining—it loses all its luster. I'm terrified of it myself.

I happen to have been married most of my life so

far to two men—one at a time, of course. I don't say I particularly minded either situation because I'm a very adaptable woman—I'm prepared to go along with a gag no matter how miserable it is. I did not marry either time for security, protection, prestige, or for a family. I married so young both times that I really had no such plans. The first time, I married only because at that time it was considered the smart thing to do. Everybody thought I was getting married, so I got married. Later I wondered, *why did I get married just because people expected me to?* Not that I wasn't fond of my husband. I was. But I really hadn't *wanted* to marry him, and I was proven right when the whole thing broke up in no time flat. The second time I didn't *want* to get married either. I did it because circumstances during World War II made it much more convenient to be married than not to be married. So you see, both times I married *because*. And the men I married probably also did it *because*. Nobody really wanted to then. We lived in a world where we didn't think marriage was the ultimate answer to anything. And it wasn't —as was shown in our case—in both cases.

What's more, I don't believe it's the ultimate answer today either. There must be a better answer. There should be a better answer. Or else women and men must come up with some better reasons for getting married at all.

14 { MARRIAGE IS NOT ADVISABLE

Throughout life, practically everybody seeks advice from all sides. From the time you're a tiny child you ask your school friends, your parents, your brothers and sisters, your uncles and aunts, your pals down at the corner and the maids in the kitchen or anybody you can grab, for advice and information. And if you think back on it you may find you never took any of it, ever, under any circumstances. One remembers many of the wise remarks that were made to one but one very seldom acts on them.

The same thing seems to me to apply to love and marriage. How many youngsters have gone to their parents and said, "Don't you think so-and-so is the most wonderful person in the world and don't you think I ought to marry him?" and the parents said,

"Absolutely not! You're too young. He can't support you." Or, "You haven't had a chance at life yet." Or whatever the parents care to say. And the youngster goes right out and does it anyhow. That's usually how much good advice does.

Really the basic advantage of seeking advice is that it gives you a chance to air your own opinions in a louder voice than you'd use if you were talking to yourself in your bathroom. A lot of people do manage to talk out loud in their bathrooms but most people only mutter, and as a result they don't hear their own thoughts quite as distinctly as they would if they said them right out loud at the dinner table. Aside from that, it's not much good asking your parents' advice because by the time you're grown up you usually despise your parents' advice. You've looked at them and decided they haven't done too well—especially in having you—and also you're not too sure their marriage is the smash hit you want yours to be.

Actually, I don't think anybody really takes the advice of anyone else. People do just what they were going to do, but they like somebody else to either back them up or to antagonize them to the point where they will do exactly the opposite to spite them. This applies especially to the advice of friends. Many women will go to their friends and say, "Do you know what he did to me now? He beat

148

me!" Or, "He didn't show up for three nights!" Or, "He spent all my father's money!" (It really doesn't matter what the particular problem is. It's always basically the same thing—a mutual dislike that's grown over a period of getting to know each other.) And the friends will say, "Oh, how terrible! Why don't you leave him?" But those women won't leave their husbands no matter what anyone says until they're ready to do so. And then it won't be because of anyone's advice. It will be because the time has come and they've had all they can take.

You've probably had that experience when your friends have come to you for advice. After you've put in your bright little witticisms and told your friends what you thought they ought to do they usually agree with you entirely but later you learn they did exactly the opposite. I have never yet given advice to a friend that was taken. (Thank heavens for that because I wouldn't want to be responsible for anybody else making a mess of a bad situation—I'd far rather she did it on her own.) Often through the years a woman friend would come to me and tell me her sad plight and ask what to do. And I would advise her, saying, "Yes, you certainly should lock him out because after all, who would let a beast like that come into one's home?" To which she would agree, "Of course! I shall never again let that beast back into my house." And the next thing I knew, they both were cutting me dead because the beast was back in the house and they were madly in love and terribly happy together again. So I've learned not to give real advice now. I just agree. A person tells you something because she's worried, and because you're her friend you should try to provide her with what she wants—at that moment. If two days later your friend wants something different in advice from you, who are you to argue about it? It's up to you to go on sympathizing. That's what a friend is for—to go on agreeing even if she hears a different story every day.

Zsa-Zsa Gabor and I never could have been friends for twenty years if I hadn't always agreed with her. She will tell me, "I've met the only man in the world I could love." I've heard that once or twice before. Then she tells me, "I can't bear this marriage. I must get a divorce." Or she says, "I've met the most wonderful man you've ever seen," and she introduces him to me, but three days later when I ask about him, she says, "Oh, him! I can't bear him!" It's not for me to say, "Now wait a second. The other day you said—" I'm not putting her on trial. It's up to me to say, "I'm so sorry he turned out no good." Or if he's turned out to be good again, "Oh darling, I'm so thrilled for you. I'm so glad you're happy."

Confiding in others is a part of life. We've

learned to speak and we're not going to unlearn it and obviously we're not going to stop telling each other little tidbits and having the glee of unloading our burdens on someone and having the peculiar joy of seeing a surprised face saying, "Oh no, you can't mean that! You must be putting me on!" But actually, nothing is more foolish than telling your innermost secrets to your women friends. Because, first of all, no matter how you tell them in the strictest confidence, it's bound to slip out—at least to one other person. Also if you're capable of telling one person, you're probably going to tell another and another and you'll tell it a little differently each time depending on the audience. When you're angry and hurt it's a great relief to get the ear of a sympathetic girl friend and say, "Imagine what that swine did to me—" You want someone to agree, "I don't know why you put up with it as long as you did." But it would be better if you had to boil in oil all by yourself, for then you might be inclined to wonder, *Did I do right? Was I fair? Am I the one in the wrong? Perhaps I've been a rotten wife.*

So when it comes to advice about marriage, your parents are squares who obviously don't know anything about it and you wouldn't take their advice in any case. Your friends are not trustworthy and besides are as ignorant as you are. Then, possibly, you seek so-called professional advice. This comes in

151

various forms or packages. The advisor could be a minister who, if he's a Catholic minister, has never been married because he's not allowed to marry and so knows absolutely nothing about marriage—or at least *should know nothing* about the problems of marriage other than hearsay, which isn't even accepted in a court of law. Or it could be a doctor who's probably had one marriage that's not too successful but he isn't going to tell you about it. Next comes the psychiatrist and marriage counselor.

Someone once described to me what a psychiatrist can do for you. She said, "The first thing he does is get rid of your husband completely." This is because most psychiatrists assume if you have a major problem in your life it's probably caused by the person you live with and once they can break that up, they've cured you. And it's true that several people I know have, after going to psychiatrists, gotten divorced and gone on to happier and merrier times. It very well may be that a lot of people are worn down by the misery of an unhappy marriage without realizing that is what their real problem is. When they do realize it, there's a completely proper court of appeals which is called the marriage counselor.

I must admit I have never consulted a marriage counselor and I would like to keep it that way. I've heard several of them on radio and television and

I've had personal reports on several of them, and have thus learned they're usually rather square people without a great deal of experience in the marriage field personally. They certainly have listened to many tales of woe and they've usually tried to explain that the fault doesn't lie entirely on one foot. That's exactly what you don't want to hear when you are embittered by the dreadful way you've been treated. What you're looking for is a little balm for your ego. You're looking for somebody to say, "Oh, you poor kid! You were absolutely right!" When you go to a marriage counselor hoping he will confirm your worst fears and explain to you what a beast your husband has been or what a wretched swine your wife is, and he says instead, "Well, you know there are two sides to every crumpet," it's inclined to turn your heart to ice. You know there are no two sides to this particular question, only to everybody else's.

Marriage counselors also serve the purpose of allowing you to loudly voice your complaints to each other. I think it's agreed among psychiatrists that the louder you complain to each other as a husband and wife team, the better clarification you'll get of your difficulties. You also will lose all sense of romance, all sense of mystery, and you both will know for sure how much the other hates you. The secret of happy relationships between people has always

153

seemed to me that you say only as much as you need to say to prevent yourself from getting a bleeding ulcer. And at the same time you avoid saying the provoking things you never can take back and which will prove that you are filled with black resentment. Psychiatrists recommend that this resentment be brought out on display almost every evening. They advise, once you are alone together in your bedroom, you tell him just how much you despise him, how you can't bear the way he eats with his mouth open, and he tells you how he loathes you and can't bear the way you slop around with your underslip sagging beneath your skirt. Whatever the quarrel is about, the psychiatric aim is to bring things out into the open so that level-headed discussion (as if there were such a thing between people emotionally involved with each other) can take place and level-headed decisions, as to how to work them out in the future, can be made.

It's always been a mystery to me how a level-headed discussion can produce worthwhile results in a sexually maladjusted marriage or how a level-headed discussion will work out a mass of debts incurred by him at the race track. I don't think it's necessarily true that airing one's grievances whisks them away. I think one's grievances are often quite real and impossible to whisk. Probably smoldering hotly without speech doesn't help matters, but I doubt that opening up and letting the other person know exactly how badly you feel about him is going to aid the situation either. At any rate the basic aim of counselors seems to be to have two people sit down and explain why they hate each other: she had an affair with the milkman; he banged his secretary. Or if it hasn't got to that point, maybe he is pretty stingy with the weekly cash and drinks it all on the way home on Saturdays and belts her a couple, or she is a slovenly, lousy housekeeper who never washes up the kitchen. The bathroom smells pretty high and bad, or she has her mother around all the time advising both of them, or whatever on earth it is that has brought things to such a head—often a mutual dislike of their own children. So, they put it all down on the counter for all the world to see while they discuss it in a clear-headed manner and presumably the clear-headed counselor, one who has never had such problems of his own, (probably being a homosexual who has never married), decides to work out how these two maladjusted people can go home and get along together.

The best thing he can point out to them really, is that they may be just as badly off when they're each on his own. For one thing, the man will have to support the children—if he can be found—and also will have to do his own laundry and get his own breakfast and endure a few other minor inconveniences which he may find less desirable than staying home, saving the cash and having a regular sex mate at any time he cares to put a finger on her, to put it crudely. She, in turn, will lose her regular escort and companion, such as he may be, and, also, a man around the house to squash large insects and replace blown fuses. The facing of these cold, true facts may result in a stalemate in which the couple decides to plow on for another few years. I don't know exactly what the statistics are on people who have visited marriage counselors, how many of them have managed to make it through life or how many have only struggled along for another eighteen months, had one more baby, or even two, to add to the problem. Some of them even may have stuck it out until the last youngster left school, but if it has resulted in happier people, I don't know.

I don't think that immature people leaping out of one marriage into another have much of a hope. Getting along with somebody is tough in any case and the fact that you failed once probably means you'll fail again. Struggling to be more realistic in your claims on another person is not very attractive or glamorous but it's entirely necessary if you're to make a go of marriage. There is no such thing as the perfect mate who does everything exactly right after the first year of marriage. Naturally, when you don't really know a person, when you're nervous

156

and struggling, everything seems far more exciting and interesting and titillating than it will eighteen months later. Five children later, it's really a very different story and to the woman who has those five children and a large case of disillusion about her husband, the idea of a new soulmate who would only want to talk about her seems a very romantic proposition—only he just doesn't exist. And the father who has a large batch of children may still see himself as the carefree young guy he was when he left school and foolishly got himself into this mess, and try to start all over again. What they both usually do is hop into exactly the same situation again with another team.

How many men because of divorce have two, three, even four families? They may lay just one egg with each wife, then they go on and repeat the same situation. And what's more, they continue to dislike it exactly as they did with the first wife. Each wife may look different but often they even look alike, and the other circumstances are alike also. No amount of marriage counseling is going to change that. A counselor may agree that there's a basic hatred between a couple and therefore advise they separate for the sake of the children so the children won't have to hear the filthy things the parents think of each other. (As if they're going to be spared that on the Saturday or Sunday Daddy takes them to the zoo. He'll certainly let fly with, "Your mother is the type of woman who—" And no matter how brave and clever a woman you are, no doubt you will give out a slightly biased version of Father's character.) Or the counselor may suggest that the couple give it another try. I always feel that the people who do go back together after consulting a counselor are merely using him as an excuse to re-unite. They wanted to stay together in the first place. People who really want to break apart go to a counselor only because they want him to say it would be better for them and the family to do so.

At best, a marriage counselor is like a friendly clergyman or a new family friend who seems to have one's interests at heart—for a fee. The confiding type of person probably will confide in anybody and everybody, listening intently to his own words and never to the replies. The non-confider will only spill the beans to his secretary or in his shower while commiserating with himself. There is a great emphasis nowadays on the value of "talking it out." It comes under the heading of communication. My own belief is that you can talk yourself right out of a love affair if you aren't careful. You can dissect it so far that there's nothing left. There is a lot to be said for the good old mystery—the long flannel nightie with a bit of fumbling attached—and the man who spent most of the week on the road while the woman stayed at home and wondered. Or better still, filled in her time with somebody more accessible. There was less talk and more action then.

15 { MARRIAGE IS THE
FIRST STEP TOWARD DIVORCE

I've forgotten exactly what the statistics are on divorce, but I think it's something like 90% of all married people today will sooner or later hit the divorce courts, either once, twice or more. Well, if those statistics are wrong, somebody's bound to have the right ones. At any rate, they are enormous. The divorce courts all over the country, not to mention all over the world except in the Catholic countries, are jammed—and I think it's a growing menace.

There are no smart ways of avoiding the divorce problem. You are always reading about people who have separated and are trying to work out their difficulties. Sometimes they succeed for a while; they go back together just because they miss each other. But, once the rift is there, they either separate

161

regularly once a year until a final break or they settle down to the grim monotony of being unhappy and accepting it. Getting along with the people you love is pretty difficult and getting along with people you don't love is darn well impossible, except by smothering one or other of the parties. Come to think of it, that's really a good idea if one could get away with it legally.

There have been many manuals written on divorce, its outcome and its traumatic effect on the participants. But nobody has ever come up with a solution other than the suggestion that we all get back to the churches and respect family life more, as if there's any going back. The main effort seems to be a wish to find a simple solution to avoid legal battles and of course a method of making fathers pay for the upkeep of their young.

So far, the law has not found a simple solution for anything, so it's not likely to find one for so desperately emotional an experience as divorce. People who have once loved each other and owned each other are most unlikely to suddenly become calm and collected when discussing the dividing of their ash trays and other goodies. It's in the nature of man never to want anyone to touch that which he has touched. After all, his mark is upon it and therefore it's his, and after he's finished with it, it should be eaten at the dinner table. But he can

162

hardly roast his wife for a Christmas dinner, not with the mores of our society, so he has to pay her off and live through the agony of knowing that some other fellow is drinking the booze he paid for and enjoying the bed he left. She feels the same. Here she is wiping the dirty noses and tending the bitten fingernails of his young while he is having a wonderful time, probably driving a sports car. It's easy to see the cause of the hatred. Nothing is going to change human nature. How on earth can a first wife enjoy the sight of a second wife wearing a fur coat that should have been hers? She certainly can't help indulging in greedy speculation as to how much he is spending on somebody else. Nor can he avoid the horrible pipe-dream of visualizing her having the pleasure of another fellow's company.

A split in one's human relations usually results in a split in one's egocentric view of oneself. Many people may not recognize it but most of them feel it, the sense of defeat, the realization that although they didn't make too much effort at the time they failed, life didn't give them a fair shake, and the going was just too rough for one poor little woman or one poor little man. Humans don't like being uprooted and they don't like changing their names much. They don't really like moving from house to house. There is a strong nesting instinct and the human being tends to try and settle down physically

163

while emotionally he never settles down. So the fact of having to pack up one's worldly possessions and move is a ghastly experience. Secondly, to pay a lawyer for getting rid of someone who cost practically nothing to acquire is hell on earth. The frightfulness of discussing one's most intimate relations and trying desperately to make them sound as if all the evil is on the other side, leaves people taking overdoses of sleeping pills, Vodka and psychiatric care. None of these things are solutions. Only a new mate and the same situation again will pacify most divorcees and divorced men.

Marriage in its peculiar way prepares for marriage. Many people who have been married twice make pretty good mates the third time because they are inured to suffering, their expectations are considerably lower and they are darn well resolved not to go through a divorce again. It's a well known fact according to Cosmopolitan and other informed women's magazines that the divorced man is a far more likely prey for a new marriage than the unmarried bachelor, and the previously wed woman is more than eager to have another go at it. However, I've been told by many men that the worst companion possible is the woman who is just going through a divorce. She has absolutely only one thing on her mind—what a beast he was, how she hates him, how she wants him back, how she put up with so much from him, how she suffered and how little he cares. The man involved is inclined to do the same thing if he can capture a sympathetic ear. The time to snare the divorced man or woman is, as Louise Rhona would put it, after they get well on someone else. Her theory in *The Divorcee's Handbook* is that every divorced person must recover on a new love. Yet that love often never lasts the night. There are too many complaints to listen to.

How comforting it must be for lawyers knowing, when they've managed to put asunder that which costs two dollars to put together, they may be pretty sure another big break will be coming their way in a few years time. In fact, for anyone whose son doesn't know what business to go into, divorce law is probably as good a bed as any for making money. The lawyer has no reason to see the couple get back together again because his fee would be much smaller, if not nonexistent. So, his first move is to encourage the wife or husband not to contact the other party at all but always to deal through him— which in itself is offensive to people who have been living in an intimate relationship for several years. "Don't discuss the children which you begot together with anyone but your lawyer," he says. He will hand the news on. This is a good chance to secure the everlasting hatred of husband for wife and wife for husband. If they should get together and say a few kind words to each other or weep into a Martini, there's a horrible chance they might call off the divorce—and this no self-respecting lawyer can allow. There always are some lonely nights when separated husbands and wives might swallow their pride and call each other. But, they know if they do, they'll never dare face their lawyer again because he'll be furious and might even order them out of the office.

A lawyer, when approached by a person seeking a divorce, has two things to think of: how good and interesting or long and boring the case is going to be, and how much money is involved. Usually it's the man who has the money, therefore lawyers prefer to represent men, but if it's the woman who comes to them, they have no choice. In this case, the smart lawyer immediately contacts the husband's lawyer. They have lunch together, pat each other on the back, promise to send each other more business in the future, and carve up the gold between them. This is common practice on a very small scale as well as on a large scale.

In most big divorces in states like California where the court tends to award the wife half of the community property—i.e., that which has accrued in the course of the marriage regardless of the state of the marriage—the lawyer can be pretty sure the woman is going to get at least what the law provides, so it isn't too much of a struggle. However, he's not going to get half or even ten percent of it unless he can create rather a stir and make the case a difficult one. Therefore, it's part of the lawyer's job to complicate the matter as much as he can or to make a deal with the husband's lawyer. It all depends on how eager the man is to get rid of his wife or how stupid he is with his money. My own experience was very enlightening.

I went to my own so-called family lawyer at that time, inasmuch as my husband had already engaged Jake Ehrlich in San Francisco. Jake Ehrlich was a well-known criminal lawyer, so obviously he was a good choice for our case. We went to court first on a separate maintenance deal and I learned to my amazement that the lawyers were asking $25,000 apiece plus $15,000 for my husband's accountant. Since they could see there was no cash in the bank, they wanted to borrow these fees against the childrens' trust fund. I won't go into all the horrible details of how they tried to bully me in the Judge's chamber to sign the paper to allow this. But the net result was I argued so long that tea time came around—or was it Martini time?—and the Judge broke up the session saying they would have to dictate the order and send it to me to sign. I never signed it, though that meant I got no maintenance for three-and-a-half months until we went to court again, but it did give me a chance to fire my lawyer. (James paid him $10,000 for his trouble in the matter.)

I hired my next lawyers, telling them what had happened in the previous instance and offering to pay them then and there $2,500 for which they claimed they could get me a divorce. Immediately afterward, they nipped up to see Jake Ehrlich in San Francisco and got an agreement for $10,000 from him, which they subsequently collected. Although I made them return my $2,500, I did not go to court with them. About that time I was getting into a state of great despair because I figured all lawyers were totally untrustworthy and that none of them were ever going to fight for me to get a reasonable deal. After all, I had been married for twenty-three years which is suffering enough.

So I decided to take the bull by the horns and go into court to represent myself. I couldn't see how I could do any worse than the others had been doing and at least I wasn't going to charge $10,000 out of our community property. Then too, neither the Judge nor anyone else could bribe me, since I loved me and was representing me. Also I figured that possibly I would make the front page of *Time* or *Life* magazines as the only Hollywood divorcee who defended herself in court and tore the whole lot of them limb from limb. But when I started looking at some of the forms, I realized I didn't understand the whereases and the here-in-unders and the insofars, and I knew I would get into a chaotic state of nerves trying to make heads or tails of what the Judge was saying, and coping with the interruptions I would be sure to get from Ehrlich or his forty-two assistants. So, secretly, I began thinking about hiring another lawyer.

I needed an able man, for there were several matters of contention in this divorce. The house, the various properties and the custody of the children which was a major issue. Since my about-to-be-ex was living in Switzerland, I didn't want the children to be wandering around that country for half the year and return to me for the other half, ruined. I was perfectly willing to bring worse charges than "mental cruelty" having been divorced many years before in England where a spade is called a spade. I was quite prepared to face the same realities here, even though such action is considered very bad form because Hollywood does not like open charges. Bread crumbs in the bed are the most extreme thing you can accuse anybody of and still be a gentleman. But then I was not attempting to be a gentleman.

At a dinner party the Christmas before, given by Marika Abba, I'd met a rather dashing young lawyer who intrigued me with tales of how he had won a U. S. Supreme Court Decision (though not in a divorce case of course) and had established a new legal precedent. He didn't seem the standard Hollywood slick talker. He waved his arms around when he was discussing things and had rather loud opinions on practically everything. He also had a fairly cozy manner; he confided; he charmed; he lied occasionally and was suitably abashed when he was caught. I decided he looked like a fairly good bet.

It turned out he was a far better bet than I could have dreamed about. His name was and is Marvin Mitchelson and he knew a great deal about real estate but hadn't concentrated particularly on divorce. I had him come to see me. I told him how I hated, despised and loathed all lawyers, distrusted them with every ounce of me, and he swore undying faithfulness, total honesty and many other things that I knew couldn't be believed. However, I engaged him and we agreed to keep it a secret and throw it at the enemy at the last moment. Actually, we only consulted for about three weeks and he did an absolutely marvelous job. He went to the enemy and told them I was totally insane and could not be reasoned with, which is what I had wanted him to do, and we won all our points hands down. Not as easily as it sounds because we had to subpoena forty witnesses, all of whom showed up in the courtroom on the day of the divorce. But James did not—

because his lawyers had taken him off a plane and hidden him somewhere in the wild hope that they might manage to get a settlement at the last minute. Well, Marvin got a settlement. More than I asked for. In fact, we turned back a few properties we couldn't be bothered to keep track of.

Marvin and I have been closely associated ever since. I sent several of my divorcing friends to him, all of whom were wildly delighted with the results. (Also he won the case I had against Loretta Young for firing my daughter Portland from a TV show. In fact, every time we've gone to court together, it's worked out well.) I must say, though I distrust most of the legal profession and advise everybody to do the same, every so often, provided you level with the lawyer and aren't afraid of hurting his feelings, you have quite a good chance he may play straight with you. But you have to keep after him; temptations are much too great when the other side comes to call. Remember, the lawyer you're dealing with is only a man.

The major contention in most divorces, where there are children, is the children themselves. Divorce really doesn't matter so much from the point of view of the couple involved, but it is tiresome for the children. Why we should consider them when they rarely consider us, I don't know—but it's an old-fashioned habit. Both parties usually claim

171

to love them madly and want to take complete charge of them, even though the man is not in the least able to, since he presumably is going to have to work for their support. The Judge almost always awards the children to the mother anyway. She'd have to have been caught in a really nasty piece of dilettanting to lose custody of her children, or else, be too ill to maintain them. The court does try to be generous with visitation rights though, and here is where a great many problems are created. Most mothers are angry just after a divorce, but realize there's nothing that can be done about it. You can't switch the father of your children after you've had them. You have to allow the brute to see them for their sake as well as his. But how this is done is a matter which should be gone into very carefully. There's nothing more aggravating for a woman who now is on her own attempting to build a new life than to have the ex dropping in and out whenever it suits him, sitting around drinking her liquor which he's glad to do since he thinks he paid for it, and stopping anybody else from visiting her. I always think it's a wise thing to make father pick up the children and take them out. It means that every moment they spend with their father is pure fun, and at home, they have to do their homework and wash behind the ears for mother. One has to fight the battle of making them like you as much as the guy who took them to Disneyland. Yet, that's better than having him hanging around the house and driving you mad.

It's all very well for me to talk. I haven't enforced that rule completely myself on account of the fact that I was fooled into thinking he would be living abroad and only visiting this country about two weeks a year. Those two weeks do spread out. Every so often I'll walk into my home and find this strange man eating or drinking in my kitchen or playing chess in the library. At first, it's so maddening you don't know whether to hurl him out and risk infuriating your children or whether to try and endure it and leave the house yourself. It gets to be even more embarrassing when you find that you have another man in your life. Even if your ex is just sneering down his nose at your new romance, your new romance is wild with rage at the sight of your ex. "Why don't you get him out of here?" he'll say. Then you say, "But the children—" Well, your new romance isn't that keen on the children either for that matter. "Why don't you get him *and* the children out?"

There are a lot of problems that face the divorcing mother. In fact, if you're thinking of ever getting a divorce, don't have any children. It makes it much simpler. The marriage may last longer and the problems when you split up are merely the stainless steel and a few torn sheets. Custody of the car really is no problem compared with custody of the children.

One of the big pitfalls is that the smart child soon realizes there's a great advantage in the enmity between his father and mother and he can sway them one way or the other and pose as the pathetic little thing in the middle. Both parents will vie to buy him things, bribe him into loving them. They can't help it because they hate each other so much. It isn't every child who catches on to this because many children are extremely heartbroken at the split-up between their parents and are devoted to both parties. But there sometimes is that shrewd little item who recognizes that this could be a pretty good thing for him. He might even become a bookie in school with the aid of his father's financing, and it's hard for a father to resist such propositions, knowing what it would do to the mother if she found out. Also there are marvelous things he can buy a boy—bicycles, motorcycles, anything that may result in a ghastly accident. And look how mother looks, the kill-joy! "You're too young to be out on a Honda." "You shouldn't be smoking marijuana, no matter what your father says." Naturally a child learns to despise that mother, and father becomes such a good sport. In some cases, the boot is on the other leg. The mere outing to Marineland becomes a farce of sheer boredom for the child who has everything and has been everywhere, thanks to mother. Poor old dad. Who cares about going to Wil Wright's for an ice cream when we have them sent in every afternoon with double barrels of fudge on them—hot! It's sad that parents will compete because of personal hatred and use the child as the lever to obtain their small satisfactions. It may seem pleasurable to a woman who thinks her husband has been stingy to force him into huge expenditures on the children. Very gratifying, but, then, what about them later on? And yet, why should one worry at all about children when like as not later on, no matter what, they'll all be at love-ins and other such remarkable activities of the times?

16 { MARRIAGE IS AN IMPERMANENT WAVE

If you examine nature at all, you see that everything in nature has a regular up-and-down, turning-around and tide. The tide comes in and it goes out every twenty-four hours—or it may be twice in twenty-four hours for all I know. The wind changes; the sun comes up, then goes down; the air is dry, a cloud bursts and there is rain. The whole of nature is a changing process. Every growing creature reaches maturity, bumps along for a while, drops off and dies. Every vegetation does the same. Flowers bloom for a few days and they look just gorgeous, then they wither and die and that's it. They have their budding and their blooming and their fading, and that is their life. That's the life of all natural things, including man.

Only man is fighting it. Man asks of the world and of nature and of his culture that he be allowed to be perpetually happy somehow and, to attain this, he uses all kinds of instruments—like music fashioned after jungle drums; he uses sedatives; he uses pep pills; he uses drugs; he uses alcohol; he uses tobacco; he uses sex. And, he uses every other wretched thing he can find: fast cars, race horses, gambling, anything in the book that may help him attain "happiness." He probably has noticed, though he doesn't want to accept it, that it all is temporary—a brief fling. Sex is spectacular for the moment, then it passes and you're left with somebody in your bed that you wish wasn't there. Drugs have a very nasty after-effect. Drink has a terrible letdown and a beastily hangover. Losing money at the race track or crap table is a terrible disappointment, not to mention the embarrassment if you don't happen to have it. Buying anything you can't afford gives you only a fleeting thrill of possession. Man is always looking for a continuation of highs in emotion, a state of affairs nature has never allowed. In nature, permanence doesn't exist.

If you're a cabbage in a field, you lie there all year until somebody picks you and either eats you in a cole slaw or boils you with corned beef, or lets you rot and digs you back into the earth. A tree grows branches with green leaves; the leaves turn

178

all sorts of colors, rot and fall, and that's it. In the spring, it does the same thing all over again—but, nothing particularly exciting ever happens to a tree unless an airplane hits it. There is nothing to give a high lift to any type of vegetation life. Yet, that is the existence, for some extraordinary reason, man seeks. He's not satisfied with the fact that his life offers something far better: highs and lows. Only man has the possibility of hideous ups and downs, the rise and fall of everything, but he is terribly dissatisfied with this possibility and wants to find a method of turning himself into a cabbage or a tree. That's what the sedatives and sleeping pills are for —how to stop existing, really, for a long part of one's life.

Man apparently has more interest and pleasure in his sex life than any other living creature. Most animals are usually objecting right up to the last moment and usually right after it too. There's no lead-in, there's no lead-out. It's just the season, and the result is offspring of some sort. Man has the fun of flirting under low lights, and of wooing and sending flowers, (Oh, if only he would!) and all sorts of other good things that go with making romance romantic. We're the only creature who has romance, and we also are the only creature who can enjoy our sex relations mutually. Nevertheless, man is busy trying to take Sodium Amytal to make it last longer, thereby giving himself more heart attacks earlier than he would have had in the first place. He is inventing all kinds of perversions and villainous, hurtful and absolutely horrid things because nothing is ever good enough for man. Nothing is constant enough for him. He always wants something that will continue and be forever, which is completely opposed to the very satisfaction of his existence. If everything stayed at a constant level of pleasure, obviously it would no longer be a pleasure —it would be a long dragged out bore. Pleasure, joy and delight come and go, and if they don't come and go, they are no longer pleasure, joy and delight.

So man is his own worst enemy, extremely dissatisfied with his situation because he doesn't recognize that it is *now*, this moment, that he must enjoy, and from the next one, he must look for yet another something. He constantly seeks another something to continue his pleasure, but he's always bewildered and amazed to find it doesn't last— nothing lasts. But then, nothing is meant to.

Marriage, where it comes into man's seeking permanent happiness, naturally falls by the wayside because He and She marry with the thought that this joy they feel today while all dressed up in orange blossoms, will last throughout their lives, happily ever after, into the sunset. Anybody who has been around somewhat knows this is not likely

180

to be so, and yet the disappointment that it isn't so, often makes both parties turn and hate each other instead of being sorry for and merciful toward each other as they should be. There is that ghastly feeling that, "You have done this to me! You were the one I thought could give me permanent happiness and you've given me absolutely nothing but trouble and worry and anxiety." Which, incidentally, is man's lot on earth. I don't know where I read it but I know man is supposed to be born in loneliness and die in loneliness and spend his entire life trying to beat his own loneliness. Actually many people enjoy their loneliness but they won't admit it because it's unfashionable and always has been. Man is a herd creature and herd creatures never like to admit they are happy outside of the nest with a large group of siblings or at least a litter to romp around with, a litter of the same age group.

The actual situation that the average person finds himself in is that he is without any real ability to enjoy the moments of pleasure that his marital situation gives him because he is not interested in the moment. He is interested in the long pull. Women particularly fail in this direction. When a woman meets a man, she never sizes him up by thinking, "Maybe this would be fun for tonight," or "He might be delightful to be with," or "This is a good hour we're having." She always thinks, "Is he serious?" and "Is this going to lead anywhere?" Well, nothing with a man is serious or going to lead anywhere until it already has done so. He never knows it's going to lead anywhere. He never thinks he's looking for anyone, unless he has a batch of five children left behind by another wife, and therefore needs a woman to take over and do some chores for him. Otherwise, man is never looking in that way. He's looking for something that will cover his needs for the evening, which may mean someone to dance with, someone to go to a ballgame with, someone to eat popcorn with, someone to tell about himself, or a bed companion. Very seldom if ever is he looking for someone who will be with him until the day he dies, swearing at his bedside, "I have loved you forever." This is a female attitude only and men do not share it at all. They only get around to feeling that way when and if they meet someone they cannot live without. Most likely, they never meet someone they can't live without, but they meet someone they can't bear for anyone else to have a chance to live with.

If a couple marries because they're deeply infatuated with each other and feel the greatest thing in the world will be when they actually own each other and can be together privately for as long as they possibly want, they are looking for trouble. Probably after a few years and a few children, the woman will feel neglected and unloved in the way she once was, when he wanted to watch her dress and undress, or even combed her hair for her. He will feel he's not having the old opportunity to display his ego, which is his main consideration at all times, and, also, he is not getting the charge out of the whole thing that he once got. So they begin to wonder which of them is to blame, and they blame each other.

Neither of them is to blame. It's life; it's nature; it's the tide. Familiarity will steal the excitement of intimacy. Intimacy is a thrilling experience when stolen, peeked at or thought about, but it never stands up too well to the everyday messing around in the same bathroom. A better education would help in these matters because if people knew it, they'd be perfectly willing and aware that the big kick is a before-kick rather than a long-long-long-after-kick. I think the more puritanically a person is brought up, the more disappointed he is liable to be in his marital relationship because the expectation will have been over-built up and over-advertised, and it will end the way most intimacies end.

Love, whatever it may mean to an individual, can develop even in a marriage relationship, but love is an ebb and flow thing the same as the rest of life. It comes and it goes, and while it's with you, you may see many things that are absurd and most unattractive about somebody and still find him lovable. Then the next day, you may find the same things aggravating and irritating because you're thinking of something else and aren't ready to give attention to the thing that yesterday was so enchanting. It's the changing face of people's moods and emotions that must be taken into consideration. Everyone should have the right to say, "Today I don't feel like speaking to you, and it shouldn't offend you because I'm exercising my right of being a human being. I'm not an automaton and I can't feel the same every day." There's nothing wrong with thinking differently from one day to the next. There's nothing wrong with loving differently from one day to the next. And every married person should be aware of this.

So, though marriage often lasts longer than many relationships that aren't legally binding, it isn't an always thing. Or, at least, the happy part of it isn't going to last indefinitely or always be the same. Marriage, like everything else in man's experience, has its ups and downs, its good and bad times. The wise man or woman will go into marriage knowing this and with his mind made up to look for the high spots and enjoy them while they last, even though he knows the good wave must pass and be followed by a flat, dull, even unhappy one. But that too will pass.